FOUL DEEDS & SUSPICIOUS DEATHS
IN STAFFORDSHIRE & THE POTTERIES

FOUL DEEDS AND SUSPICIOUS DEATHS Series

Wharncliffe's *Foul Deeds and Suspicious Deaths* series explores, in detail, crimes of passion, brutal murders and foul misdemeanours from early modern times to the present day. Victorian street crime, mysterious deaths and modern murders tell tales where passion, jealousy and social deprivation brought unexpected violence to those involved. From unexplained death and suicide to murder and manslaughter, the books provide a fascinating insight into the lives of both victims and perpetrators as well as society as a whole.

Other titles in the series include:

Foul Deeds and Suspicious Deaths in Birmingham, Nick Billingham
ISBN: 1-903425-96-4. £10.99

Foul Deeds and Suspicious Deaths in Bolton, Glynis Cooper
ISBN: 1-903425-63-8. £9.99

Foul Deeds and Suspicious Deaths in Colchester, Patrick Denney
ISBN: 1-903425-80-8. £10.99

Foul Deeds and Suspicious Deaths in Coventry, David McGrory
ISBN: 1-903425-57-3. £9.99

Foul Deeds and Suspicious Deaths Around Derby, Kevin Turton
ISBN: 1-903425-76-X. £9.99

Foul Deeds and Suspicious Deaths in & around Durham, Maureen Anderson
ISBN: 1-903425-46-8. £9.99

Foul Deeds and Suspicious Deaths in Hampstead, Holburn & St Pancras, Mark Aston
ISBN: 1-903425-94-8. £10.99

Foul Deeds and Suspicious Deaths in Hull, David Goodman
ISBN: 1-903425-43-3. £9.99

Foul Deeds and Suspicious Deaths Around Leicester, Kevin Turton
ISBN: 1-903425-73-1. £10.99

Foul Deeds and Suspicious Deaths in London's East End, Geoffrey Howse
ISBN: 1-903425-71-9. £10.99

Foul Deeds and Suspicious Deaths in London's West End, Geoffrey Howse
ISBN: 1-845630-01-7. £10.99

Foul Deeds and Suspicious Deaths in Manchester, Martin Baggoley
ISBN: 1-903425-65-4. £9.99

Foul Deeds and Suspicious Deaths in Newcastle, Maureen Anderson
ISBN: 1-903425-34-4. £9.99

Foul Deeds and Suspicious Deaths Around Newport, Terry Underwood
ISBN: 1-903425-59-X. £9.99

Foul Deeds and Suspicious Deaths in and Around Scunthorpe, Stephen Wade
ISBN: 1-903425-88-3. £9.99

Foul Deeds and Suspicious Deaths in Stratford & S. Warwickshire, Nick Billingham
ISBN: 1-903425-99-9. £10.99

More Foul Deeds and Suspicious Deaths in Wakefield, Kate Taylor
ISBN: 1-903425-48-4. £9.99

Foul Deeds and Suspicious Deaths in York, Keith Henson
ISBN: 1-903425-33-6. £9.99

Foul Deeds and Suspicious Deaths on the Yorkshire Coast, Alan Whitworth
ISBN: 1-903425-01-8. £9.99

Please contact us via any of the methods below for more information or a catalogue.

WHARNCLIFFE BOOKS
47 Church Street – Barnsley – South Yorkshire S70 2AS
Tel: 01226 734555 – 734222; Fax: 01226 724438
E-mail: enquiries@pen-and-sword.co.uk
Website: www.wharncliffebooks.co.uk

Foul Deeds & Suspicious Deaths In
STAFFORDSHIRE
&
THE POTTERIES

NICHOLAS CORDER

Series Editor
Brian Elliott

Wharncliffe Books

First Published in Great Britain in 2006 by
Wharncliffe Books
an imprint of
Pen and Sword Books Ltd
47 Church Street
Barnsley
South Yorkshire
S70 2AS

Copyright © Nicholas Corder 2006

ISBN: 1-845630-09-2

Typeset in 11/13pt Plantin by Concept, Huddersfield.

Printed and bound in England by Biddles Ltd.

Pen and Sword Books Ltd incorporates the Imprints of
Pen & Sword Aviation, Pen & Sword Maritime,
Pen & Sword Military, Wharncliffe Books,
Pen & Sword Select, Pen and Sword Military Classics
and Leo Cooper.

For a complete list of Pen & Sword titles please contact
PEN & SWORD BOOKS LIMITED
47 Church Street
Barnsley
South Yorkshire
S70 2BR
England
E-mail: enquiries@pen-and-sword.co.uk
Website: www.pen-and-sword.co.uk

Contents

Acknowledgements

I am deeply indebted to the patient help of the library staff throughout Staffordshire, and most especially at the William Salt Library in Stafford, Shire Hall Library in Stafford and the Stoke-on-Trent Archives in Hanley.

A huge thanks to Ivor Davies for reading the manuscript, even as it spooled out of my printer. As ever, my wife Pauline did all the household chores while I was up to my armpits in this book. She also acted as research assistant, typist, secretary, carrier of the bags, cracker of the whip, and made 17,328 cups of coffee.

If I have forgotten to thank anyone who helped, then I can only apologise.

Introduction

Changes in county boundaries over the years always make it difficult to know exactly what qualifies as 'Staffordshire'. For example, until recently it included parts of Wolverhampton. Historically, even suburbs of Birmingham were part of the old shire. Boundaries change, and for the sake of keeping to a tight geographical area, I have chosen to use the modern county of Stafford, with the unitary authority of Stoke-on-Trent, as the area covered by this book.

The northern extremity – what is loosely called Stoke-on-Trent by those from outside the district (inaccurately, to local minds) – was once an area of coal mines and the manufacture of pottery. The towns that made up the area each had its own separate identity – still recognised by those who live there, but which is not apparent to the casual observer. Just as Georgian London was segregated from nearby Islington by farmland, so were these bustling industrial centres separated by fields – long since gone as one town gradually blended into the next.

Elsewhere in the county, Stafford was a shoemaking town, Lichfield a busy Cathedral city, Burton-on-Trent famed for its beer, and the Staffordshire part of the West Midlands dominated by engineering and heavy industry. However, large swathes of Staffordshire were, and still are, largely rural, especially the Moorlands, which fringe the Peak District. Staffordshire has always mixed industry and agriculture, and to the extent that these two activities exist anywhere in modern Britain, still does to this day.

The canals brought prosperity to the Potteries, ceramic goods being less prone to breakages when transported by water than by packhorse. Then the railways opened the whole world to Staffordshire goods and industry, many of which – such as Wedgwood Pottery and Burton Ales – became world-renowned. The canal and the railway both feature in different crimes in this book, which essentially covers misdeeds committed in the eighteenth and nineteenth centuries.

In those days, the detection of crime was a haphazard business. Until 1842, Staffordshire had no professional police force, such as we would recognise, and relied on a system of 'constables' that had essentially sprung out of the Norman system of government. And when the county did get a police force, it was not the crisp, efficient, well-oiled machine one might have expected. The 200 men originally recruited for the new force had been reduced by almost half, mainly through discharges and dismissals, within the space of two years. To say that it was a force above corruption, or even the suspicion of corruption, would be generous in the extreme.

Alongside this new form of policing various associations sprang up, largely consisting of local dignitaries (the 'great and the good', or if you prefer the 'rich and the noisy'), whose members were dismayed by the 'upsurge' in crime and encouraged the reporting of criminals to the authorities by offering rewards. Some of these existed into the early part of the twentieth century. Burslem's Association for the Prosecution of Felons aimed 'to bring Offenders of every description to condign punishment.' If someone you reported for stealing coal from carts was convicted, you could earn £5 5s (over £300 in modern money). But reporting a highway robbery was much more lucrative at £20 (over £1,000 today).

How effective these incentives were is open to conjecture. One suspects that many unpopular innocents were reported for the good money on offer, if indeed they were reported at all. In fact, the *Staffordshire Sentinel* of Saturday, 31 January 1880, records a quiet year for one Potteries' Association in the following terms:

> *The Hanley Association for the Prosecution of Felons has had nothing in particular to do this year except dine – which it did on Thursday in a thoroughly efficient and satisfactory manner. The fact that the Society has had nobody to prosecute during the year no more proves that it has existed in vain than the fact that a man's house has not been burnt down, proves him a fool for having insured it.*

It's good to know the fear of coal being stolen from carts didn't upset their digestive systems!

The dispensing of justice was quick, if not always just. Often a complex murder case would be heard in a matter of a couple of hours. Hearsay, opinion and conjecture were often enough to convict. Juries (all male, of course) might take only minutes to come to a verdict. Interestingly, the trial of William Palmer (see Chapter 11) was the first case to be tried elsewhere in the country to avoid local bias.

At the centre of any history of criminal misdeeds in Staffordshire is Stafford Gaol. At least 106 hangings took place at the gaol between 1793 and 1914. The crimes for which men, women, and even children were hanged included horse stealing, 'uttering forged note' (counterfeiting money), housebreaking, assault and robbery, as well as murder – although in Sarah Westwood's case (see Chapter 8), this was relegated to 'administering arsenic'.

Until the mid-nineteenth century, hanging took place in public. If this was to discourage others, it never worked. The hangmen were often themselves criminals and less-than-competent. They drew large crowds that blocked Stafford's roads, eager to catch a glimpse of the latest victim of the hangman's noose. Among the crowds were ballad-sellers, purveying abominable doggerel that told the tale of the wrongdoer's misdeeds, often pretending they were telling a cautionary tale but really muckraking in the great British tradition. As spectators jostled for the best view of a hanging, they were regularly worked over by pickpockets. Until 1861, if caught, they too faced capital punishment: although in practice this was often commuted to transportation or imprisonment. So much for deterrence.

This book contains stories that include serial killing, crimes of passion, petty domestic disputes with spectacularly tragic consequences, self-harm, wrongful arrest and miscarriages of justice. Some of the stories have been written about often. William Palmer, the Rugeley Poisoner, is well-known, and became the subject of a TV drama a few years ago. Similarly, the story of Christina Collins (see Chapter 6) formed the basis of one of Colin Dexter's *Inspector Morse* novels. The George Edalji Case (see Chapter 19) was recently used in a novel by Julian Barnes, and while well-documented, it does not have the notoriety it perhaps deserves. The case was an appalling mis-carriage of justice, based purely on racial intolerance. It was, in essence, the British equivalent of the Dreyfus case, and should be part of the National consciousness. Interestingly, Palmer (a hard-drinking serial killer) and Edalji (a hard-working lawyer) attended the same small school, although they were not con-temporaries. Other protagonists are less well-known, but include perverts, swindlers, cheats, psychopaths and victims of injustice. Many of the crimes were born of alcohol abuse, madness, mistake, greed, fear and jealousy. Several of the misdeeds in this book are typical of those committed in any large urban sprawl where overcrowding and living hand-to-mouth are the norm. Although many of Staffordshire's large employers were enlightened by the standards of the day, poverty was routine when many of these crimes were com-mitted. However, crime is not the preserve of the urban poor. There are three murderous doctors in this book, and many of the events described took place in villages – tiny hamlets even – where their effect must have been felt for generations.

Open today's paper and you'll see the modern equivalents. You'll also see the same platitudes on the cause of crime and how to contain it as you'd find in newspapers from over a century ago. *Plus ça change* . . .

Nicholas Corder
2006

Note on Currency Changes and Monetary Values

Before 1971 Britain had a currency system based on pounds, shillings and pence. In this system, 12 pennies (abbreviated to '*d*' for 'denarius' or 'denarii', the Latin terms for 'penny' and 'pence', respectively) made 1 shilling (abbreviated to '*s*'), and 20 shillings made 1 pound (£). Other coins included: a florin, worth 2 shillings; a half-crown, worth 2 shillings and 6 pence (i.e. 2*s* 6*d*); and a guinea, worth 21 shillings. Decimalisation simplified matters considerably, scrapping all but pounds and pence, the former to be worth 100 of the latter. Thus, after February 1971, an old shilling became 5p, an old florin became 10p, an old half-crown became 12.5p, and an old guinea £1.05.

So much for the old and new systems, but what about the *value* of money in previous centuries – how has that changed? This book opens in 1700 and closes in 1919. To gain a rough idea of modern comparables for sums quoted, consider this: the value of £1 in 1700 converts to a modern equivalent of around £120; the value of £1 in 1870 converts to a modern equivalent of around £60; and the value of £1 in 1919 converts to a modern equivalent of approximately £30.

CHAPTER 1

George Caddell: Cad, Bounder, Doctor and Killer
1700

A woman who has fallen a sacrifice to the arts of one man should be very cautious in yielding to the addresses of another ...

According to the *Newgate Calendar*, George Caddell was executed for the 'Cruel Murder of Miss Price, Whom he had Seduced and Promised Marriage.'

It wasn't the first time young Miss Price had been seduced. Some years before, she'd fallen victim to the charms of an army officer, who'd left her stranded, so she'd had some practice already. Elizabeth Price was certainly resourceful and, in an era when it was not hard to be shunned for the slightest social gaffe, 'after her misfortune, supported herself by her skill in needlework.' Whether the unnamed army officer who caused her misfortune also promised marriage in order to get his wicked way is not known, but the press certainly claimed that her next Romeo did.

Miss Price's second recorded seducer was a young man by the name of George Caddell. Caddell was born in Bromsgrove in Worcestershire. He was apprenticed to an apothecary in Worcester and, when he had finished his apprenticeship, decided to add the skills of surgeon to his repertoire, moving to London to learn his trade. Some 300 years ago, the skills of a surgeon were not as finely honed and tested as they are today. According to the *Newgate Calendar*, 'As soon as he became tolerably acquainted with the profession he went to Worcester, and lived with Mr Randall, a capital surgeon of that city: in this situation he was equally admired for the depth of his abilities and amiableness of his temper.'

Here, he married his employer's daughter. How much say Mr Randall's daughter would have had in the matter is open to speculation. However, the marriage was not to last long. Soon after, Caddell's young wife died in labour with their first child.

Leaving his unhappy past behind him, Caddell moved on to the beautiful city of Lichfield, where he found himself courting the daughter of his new employer, Mr Dean. Caddell's new patron was an established surgeon in the town and Miss Dean looked like a good match for the young widower.

If it seems like a pattern is building up – move to a new town, then court the boss's daughter – it is probably mere coincide, rather than a calculated move on Caddell's part. Besides, as we shall see later from the way he acted when he eventually committed a capital crime, ruthlessness doesn't seem to have been part of his make-up. The more likely explanation is simply that his circle of acquaintance would have been fairly narrow: such matches were not uncommon. Miss Dean, as the daughter of a surgeon, would have been of the right social class to marry a man in the same profession, and would probably be to some extent schooled in the ways of looking after a surgeon and his residence, which would also have been his place of work.

However, the course of Caddell's second engagement was not to run smooth. Not far from Caddell's house lived the needleworking Elizabeth Price, who was to become his victim. According to the *Newgate Calendar*, 'Caddell becoming acquainted with her, a considerable degree of intimacy subsisted between them; and Miss Price, degraded as she was by the unfortunate step she had taken, still thought herself an equal match for one of Mr Caddell's rank of life.'

Caddell now found himself caught between an affair with a woman who was already considered to have fallen from grace and the courting of Miss Dean, who, as far as we can make out, was the perfect image of respectability. The inevitable happened. The courtship of Miss Dean would probably have been a chaste business, especially as she would have been under the watchful eye of her father. That of Miss Price would have been less closely supervised. Indeed, the 'degree of intimacy' between George Caddell and Elizabeth Price led to Elizabeth's becoming pregnant.

At around the same time, Elizabeth realised that Caddell was also wooing the Doctor's daughter. One cannot imagine her being best pleased. According to the author of the *Newgate Calendar*, 'she then became more importunate than ever, and threatened, in case of his non-compliance, to put an end to all his prospects with that young lady, by discovering every thing that had passed between them.' This was the trigger for Caddell: 'Hereupon Caddell formed the horrible resolution of murdering Miss Price; for he could neither bear the thought of forfeiting the esteem of a woman that he courted, nor of marrying her who had been as condescending to another as to himself.'

While the *Newgate Calendar* seems to indicate that it was a straight choice between a virgin and a woman who simply did too much 'condescending', Caddell's dilemma was probably greater than that. As a surgeon, he needed at least a veneer of respectability, a good name and a wife to match. It's likely that his time with Elizabeth Price was little more than dalliance. She was willing, he was willing, so they did some 'condescending'.

One can imagine that the poor girl had fallen a fair distance already and the idea of incurring yet more public scorn at her condition was too much, but whether she hoped to trap the young doctor or whether she simply wanted him to stand by her as a result of accidental pregnancy is conjecture. One thing is for sure, Elizabeth Price asked Caddell to break off his engagement to Miss Dean and marry her. If he didn't, she was prepared to tell the world precisely what their situation was.

Caddell's solution was simple enough. He would eliminate the cause of his problems:

This dreadful scheme [of murdering Elizabeth] having entered his head, he called on Miss Price on a Saturday evening, and requested that she would walk in the fields with him on the afternoon of the following day, in order to adjust the plan of their intended marriage. Miss Price, thus deluded, met him at the time appointed, on the road leading towards Burton-upon-Trent, at a house known by the sign of the Nag's Head.

As far as we know, up to the moment Caddell pulled out his knife, he had never committed another crime. The young surgeon must have been esteemed in the town, with the prospect of marriage to the daughter of a prominent surgeon endorsing public opinion. These sentiments would also have been tinged with a certain degree of pity for him as the newly bereaved widower.

As a criminal, Caddell was inept in the extreme. He knew enough about anatomy to cut Elizabeth's throat as they sat together under a tree in the middle of the fields. However, he left behind not only the knife, but his entire surgeon's instrument case. It wasn't long before both crime and perpetrator were discovered.

When he [George Caddell] came home it was observed that he appeared exceedingly confused, though the reason of the perturbation of his mind could not even be guessed at. But, on the following morning, Miss Price being found murdered in the field, great numbers of people went to take a view of the body, among whom was the woman of the house where she lodged, who recollected that she [Elizabeth] had said she was going to walk with Mr Caddell; on which the instruments were examined, and known to have belonged to him.

It was a straightforward case. Caddell was immediately taken into custody and soon transferred to Stafford Gaol. The old gaol stood at the start of Stone Road, a short distance from where the 'new' gaol now stands. Although writing nearly 80 years after the murder of Elizabeth Price, one suspects that the gaol hadn't changed a great deal by the time John Howard, the penal reformer, recorded:

Stafford. At the North Gate. Three rooms for men and two for women. A room below called the dungeon with four apertures about 4 inches square. No employment; Prisoners always shut up, and in irons; the small court not secure.

Caddell was inevitably found guilty, condemned to death, and executed at Stafford on 21 of July 1700.

While there have been more complicated cases in the annals of crime, the *Newgate Calendar* is quick to jump on the story in

Lichfield Cathedral – George Caddell walked in the fields near here before killing his pregnant mistress, Elizabeth Price. The author

order to pretend that it is a morality tale, rather than just another case of prurient interest being aroused:

> *We have no particular account of the behaviour of this malefactor while under sentence of death, or at the place of execution; yet his fate will afford an instructive lesson to youth.*

This is pretty much the line tabloid newspapers take when they reveal tales of shocking depravity, ostensibly as a lesson for their readers to avoid the traps of crime and carnality. It continues in this vein:

> *Let no young man, who has connexions of any kind with one woman, think of paying his addresses to another. There can be no such thing as honourable courtship while dishonourable love subsists. Mr Caddell might have lived a credit to himself, and an ornament to his profession, if he had not held a criminal connexion with Miss Price.*

As for what happened to Miss Price, the author of the *Newgate Calendar* decided that she was at least partially to blame for her own murder:

Her fate ought to impress on the mind of our female readers the importance of modest reserve to a woman. We would not be severe on the failings of the sex; but we cannot help observing, that a woman who has fallen a sacrifice to the arts of one man should be very cautious in yielding to the addresses of another. One false step may be recovered; but the progress of vice is a downhill road; and the farther we depart from the paths of virtue, still the faster we run. On the contrary, the ways of Virtue are pleasant; and 'all her paths are paths of peace.'

Young ladies who fall for young men aren't the only ones to receive a stern lecture either, for the author continues:

From this story likewise the young officers of our army may learn an useful lesson: for, if Miss Price had not been debauched by one of that profession, the fatal catastrophe above-mentioned had never happened.

While the modern reader would hesitate to draw these conclusions from this sad tale, what we do learn is that for all our advances in wealth, technology, medicine and social movement, human behaviour has not changed a great deal during the last 300 years: as can be seen in the stories that follow.

CHAPTER 2

A Crime of Passion
1797

*Oh William, what have I done!
What trouble have I brought
on this family and myself?*

Thomas Milward Oliver was another doctor – a profession that is well-represented in the crimes reported in this book. He had arrived in Burslem in the 1790s, where he assisted a Doctor Hickman, who had an established practice. The young Mr Oliver soon found himself much in demand, and one has the impression he was particularly popular with his female patients. One of these was the wife of a wealthy pottery manufacturer, John Wood, who owned a large property just outside Burslem, in the grounds of which was the pottery works from which he made his fortune.

While treating Mrs Wood, Doctor Oliver encountered the daughter of the family, Maria, and they became increasingly friendly – in fact, it could be said they were courting. To the wealthy industrialist John Wood, Oliver must have seemed like a bit of an upstart. Like many of the entrepreneurial middle-classes, Wood may well have had his eyes set on someone a rung higher up the social ladder – perhaps the son of another industrialist or even a minor aristocrat – as a more suitable mate for his daughter. Wood banned Oliver from seeing Maria and indeed, it is reported that on one occasion, with the ban in place, the two lovers met illicitly. When Wood stumbled across them, he and Oliver came to blows.

Oliver was then barred from the Wood's property, which he greatly resented. Then, for some inexplicable reason, when Mrs Wood fell ill again, it was young Doctor Oliver who was called to the bedside. Perhaps Dr Hickman was unavailable, or maybe in her illness, Mrs Wood demanded that she see her favourite young doctor, regardless of her husband's opinions of him. Of course, treating Mrs Wood meant that Thomas Milward Oliver and Maria could easily bump into one another, so Wood did everything he could to make sure this didn't happen while Oliver was treating his wife.

Ban an activity and it becomes all the more desirable. Thomas Milward Oliver became a man possessed. He wasn't allowed to meet Maria and his anger was plain for all to see as he vented his spleen in his local public house, *The Turk's Head*, on Bucknall Road in Burslem. Among the coterie of drinkers at *The Turk's Head* listening to Oliver's tales of lost love was a certain Ralph Johnson. The two men would often go pistol shooting together. Johnson kept several guns, as well as the equipment needed to manufacture the bullets for them – which was fairly common practice in those days. Johnson and Oliver spent the evening of the 26 January 1797 making bullets for Johnson's guns, which Oliver then proceeded to borrow.

The following morning, Oliver called at Mr Wood's house and demanded to see John Wood. He told the servants that Mr Wood owed him money for the treatment he had given Mrs Wood during her recent illness. They asked him to go to the accounts office, where one of the clerks would sort out his invoice, but Oliver insisted he wanted to present the bill to Mr Wood in person. Oliver was ushered into Mr Wood's study to wait for the Master of the House. Wood arrived a few minutes later and a shot rang out.

The Turk's Head, *Burslem – an artist's impression of the inn where Dr Thomas Milward Oliver drank regularly.* The author

At his trial, Oliver swore that his intention while waiting for Mr Wood was to commit suicide in front of him, to show him what agony he had endured since being barred from meeting Maria. However, that is not what happened. According to William Bathwell, foreman to Mr Wood, the moment John Wood entered the room, Oliver levelled a pistol at him from a distance of 3 or 4 feet and fired with the words, 'Here, do you take this!' Bathwell goes on to testify:

Mr Oliver laid the pistol down he had discharged and took the other in his right hand . . . he was fumbling with his right hand at the lock as if to cock it – it was pointed to me . . . I sprung forward, pushed the point down and seized him by the arms above the elbows . . . he held the pistol in his hand behind him and was moving it to his other hand. I slipped my hand down, knocked the pistol out of his hand, and flung him on two chairs . . . I called for the maid and directed her to take up the pistol – she was so much alarmed she durst not – when Mr Oliver found the family was alarmed, he said, 'Oh William, what have I done! What trouble have I brought on this family and myself?'

The evidence was damning, but it took the jury a good hour to find Oliver guilty. Given that Oliver had confessed to the crime and there were also reliable witnesses, this was a lengthy deliberation by the standards of the day. This hints at a certain level of sympathy, although the jury was not to be persuaded that Thomas Milward Oliver was insane at the time of the killing. According to the broadsheet, the Judge condemned Oliver with the following words:

That you, Thomas Milward Oliver, be taken to the place from whence you came, and from thence to the place of execution on Monday next, there to be hanged by the neck till you are dead, and your body given to the surgeons for dissection, and may the Lord have mercy on your soul.

The broadsheet adds that 'All present were shaken by the experience of the trial.' It does, however, reassure us with the fact that 'Such a scene, thank God, is scarcely ever seen.'

Thomas Milward Oliver seemed to arouse a mixture of prurient interest and no little sympathy. That a doctor should take a life was scandalous; that he had done it for love of an unattainable woman gave it a romantic edge. Despite his crime, he was still thought of highly. Even a broadsheet sold at Oliver's execution described him as:

> *Born of a very respectable family at Stourbridge in Worcestershire, where he received his education, and also served his apprenticeship with a surgeon and apothecary, during the whole of which period, his conduct was always that of a diligent, regular and humane young man ... At his trial, since his condemnation, and during the whole of his confinement, his behaviour has been composed, decorous and even exemplary ... he spoke of Mr Wood, the deceased, with respect and kindness and ... he was deeply concerned for the affliction he brought on Mr Wood's family.*

The whole affair certainly stirred the public's imagination. The publisher of the *Staffordshire Advertiser*, J Drewry, decided the trial of Thomas Milward Oliver was ripe for exploitation. Their newspapers carried advertisements for a pamphlet entitled, 'The trial of T M Oliver for the murder of John Wood'. It cost 1s 6d, approximately equivalent to £6 in today's money, although this would constitute a larger proportion of a working person's wage. In the booklet, the 'last moments of Mr Oliver' are recorded in the following terms:

> *On Monday morning at 10.30, the platform erected over the entrance of the New Gaol, for the execution of criminals, exhibited the most solemn and interesting scene that has occurred since the building of the prison. Mr Thomas Milward Oliver, a young man, well defended, well educated, and respectable in the exercise of a liberal profession, was then brought out to suffer death for the Murder of Mr John Wood.*
>
> *Of the deceased Mr Oliver frequently spoke in terms of great esteem; but upon all occasions he steadily and calmly denied his having formed, or felt, even for one moment, the slightest intentions against the life of Mr Wood. The same composure of mind, and the same ... firmness ... of behaviour, which he preserved during his trial, continued through the whole of that awful interval which passed between his sentence and his execution. In his conversation with the Rev. Mr Booker & the Rev. Dr Parr, who frequently*

attended him in his cell, he was often serious, but without dejection, and sometimes cheerful, but without levity. His devotion was rational and fervent; and his spirit was full of that Charity, which the great Apostle hath so luminously described, and so pathetically enforced.

On Monday morning he was engaged in most solemn discourse and private prayer, with the two friends above mentioned, and about 9.45, he came down with them into the Chapel, where the Holy Sacrament was administered to him by The Rev. Mr Dickinson, Rector of Stafford, and the Rev. Mr Rathbone, Ordinary of the Prison. It was observed that while the Services of Religion were performing, the colour of his face never changed – that his hand never shook – and that on receiving the Cup from Mr Dickinson, he shed one tear only. When his arm had been pinioned in the Gaoler's Office, he was accompanied by the Reverend Mr Booker, to the top of the Porter's Lodge, where they immediately knelt down together and repeated the Lord's Prayer. Mr Brooker, after a short condemnatory prayer, retired, and Mr Oliver, with firmness in his step, and serenity in his countenance, went up to the stage, on which he respectfully bowed to the spectators; and having stood nearly 3 minutes quite undismayed, was then launched into Eternity. His body about noon was conveyed to the Infirmary; it was opened according to the sentence of the Law by Mr Hughes, one of Surgeons of the Hospital, in the presence of Mr Fowke the Apothecary, and other Medical Assistants; and such persons as were desirous to view it were admitted through the gates of the Infirmary for that purpose.

So, not only could you get to see the famous hothead who had been thwarted in love hanged, but if you were very lucky, you could go and inspect his entrails in the Infirmary afterwards.

CHAPTER 3

George Allen: Murdering his Children
1807

The monster was found standing in the middle of the house-place with a razor in his hand ...

n the early nineteenth century, medical science not being as advanced as it is today, anyone suffering from epilepsy was not always treated with the milk of human kindness. There's a fair description of an epileptic seizure in the Bible, in St Mark's Gospel, which is defined as being a 'foul spirit', which is then cast from a boy by Jesus, after the disciples have failed to do the same trick. In the Middle Ages, the seizures associated with epilepsy were seen as evidence that a person – especially a woman – was a witch. It wasn't until 50 years or more after George Allen hanged for his crimes, that doctors began to understand the real nature of epilepsy and come up with medicines to help control the disease.

The Times headline, 'GEORGE ALLEN – An Epileptic, who was executed at Stafford, 30 March 1807, for the Murder of his Three Children' may seem offensive to modern sensibilities, but it was, perhaps, an attempt at an enlightened understanding of why a man should suddenly murder his three children. The article continues:

> *INSANITY probably caused the horrid deed to be committed which we are now going to relate. It appeared in evidence on the trial that George Allen had previously thereto been subject to epileptic fits, but that on the Sunday preceding the day whereon he committed the murder he was considerably better. Though a jury found him guilty of premeditated murder, we must, in charity to the*

failings of human nature, suppose that one of these mental derange-
ments, epilepsy, again seized him at the time he committed this
strange, cruel, and most unnatural murder. His examination before
the coroner also seems to favour this opinion.

It is much more likely that epilepsy was the symptom of some
greater illness, or perhaps the result of a head injury, but
certainly wasn't the cause of George Allen's murder spree.
Whatever the real diagnosis, the Allen case captured the
public's imagination. He hadn't merely killed one of his own
children, but *three*. This was much more intoxicating and heady
stuff than the everyday fare of poaching, highway robbery and
petty theft. This was a real crime, over which people could
agonise for years to come. It was also a good excuse for
J Drewry, publisher of the *Staffordshire Advertiser*, to publish
one of their occasional one-off specials, which they could then
advertise in their own pages. For a shilling you could read:

The Trial of GEORGE ALLEN of Upper Mayfield Who dread-
fully wounded, with intent to murder his wife! and who actually
MURDERED HIS THREE CHILDREN!!! By cutting off their
Heads, and tearing their Bowels out!! With an account of HIS
EXECUTION AT STAFFORD On Easter Monday.

As far as can be made out from contemporary reports, George
Allen was a straightforward man. He earned his living as a
labourer, living at Upper Mayfield, a cluster of houses on the
Staffordshire–Derbyshire border, not far from Ashbourne.
According to a report in the *Staffordshire Advertiser*, Allen was
a decent, hard-working man who had lived in harmony with his
wife for 17 years. Nothing untoward seemed to have happened
at all until, according to the *Newgate Calendar*:

At 8 o'clock on the evening of the 12th of January, 1807, he retired
to rest, and when his wife followed him, in the course of an hour, she
found him sitting upright in bed, smoking his pipe, which was his
usual custom. In another bed, in the same room, lay three of his
infant children asleep, the eldest boy, about 10 years old, the second
a girl about 6, and another boy about 3. When his wife got into bed,
with an infant at her breast, he asked her what other man she had
in the house with her. To which she replied that no man had been,

there but himself. He insisted to the contrary, and his wife continued to assert her innocence. He then jumped out of bed and went downstairs, and she, from an impulse of fear, followed him. She met him on the stairs and asked him what he had been doing in such a hurry. In answer he ordered her to get upstairs again. He then went to the bed where his children were and turned down the clothes. On her endeavouring to hold him he told her to let him alone, or he would serve her with the same sauce, and immediately attempted to cut her throat, in which he partly succeeded, and also wounded her right breast; but a handkerchief she wore about her head and neck prevented the wound from being fatal. She then extricated herself (having the babe in her arms all the time, which she preserved unhurt), and jumped, or rather fell, downstairs. Before she had well got up, one of the children (the girl) fell at her feet, with her head almost cut off, which he had murdered and thrown after her. The woman opened the door and screamed out that her husband was cutting off their children's heads. A neighbour soon came to her assistance, and when a light was procured the monster was found standing in the middle of the house-place with a razor in his hand. When asked what he had been doing, he replied coolly: Nothing yet, I have only killed three of them!

On their going upstairs a most dreadful spectacle presented itself: the head of one of the boys was very nearly severed from his body, and the bellies of both were partly cut and partly ripped open, and the bowels torn completely out and thrown on the floor. Allen made no attempt to escape, and was taken without resistance. He said that it was his intention to have murdered his wife and all her children, and then to have put an end to himself. He professed his intention also to have murdered an old woman who lay bedridden in the same house.

This was a crime that came from nowhere. There seemed to be no reason or motive for it, which is probably why the newspaper attempted to ascribe it to epilepsy. Was Mrs Allen's 'attempt to hold him' an attempt to stop George Allen from doing something, or was this what she did as a matter of course whenever he had a seizure, to prevent him from causing himself any damage? As far as can be ascertained, Mrs Allen had no lover and the accusation that there was another man in the house was Allen's own invention.

One possible explanation might be that Allen had, for whatever reason, begun to have hallucinations or to interpret ordinary events in such a way as to give them a strange twist. Stalkers, for instance, will interpret some day-to-day activity by their quarry as a signal: the victim draws a curtain and the stalker interprets it as a signal of the victim's love for them, rather than accepting the act for what it is – drawing a curtain to let in daylight. Perhaps some clue is available from the coroner's inquiry. As the *Newgate Calendar* reports:

> *An inquest was held on the bodies of the three children, before Mr Hand, coroner of Uttoxeter, when he confessed his guilt, but without expressing any contrition. In answer to other interrogations he promised to confess something that had lain heavy on his mind; and Mr Hand, supposing it might relate to a crime he had heretofore committed, caused him to be examined in the presence of other gentlemen, when he told an incoherent story of a ghost, in the shape of a horse, having, about 4 years ago, enticed him into a stable, where it drew blood from him, and then flew into the sky. With respect to the murder of his children, he observed to the coroner, with apparent unconcern, that he supposed it was as bad a case as ever he had heard of.*

So maybe Allen had begun to have dreams or fantasies that compelled him somehow to do this. Whatever the unusual circumstances that surrounded the case, Allen was executed outside Stafford Gaol on 30 March 1807.

CHAPTER 4

Richard Tomlinson: Murder Ran in the Family
1833

A wound at the back of the deceased's head had evidently been caused by some blunt instrument ...

In the nineteenth century, public hanging was a popular spectator sport. While a single hanging was a fair attraction, especially if the killer was particularly notorious, there was little to beat a good multiple hanging: so 19 March 1834 must have been a particularly bright day in the Stafford calendar for fans of the noose. They were to be treated to the spectacle of a triple hanging of mixed offenders – a man, a boy and a woman. There would be something for everyone.

There was even something for local preachers, one of whom had printed up a copy of a sermon entitled, 'The Watchman's Cry'. It is a rant of 8,000 words in which the congregation must have been far more impressed by the speaker's ability to go on for so long than by the rambling content. The intention seems to be that the crimes and subsequent hangings are a morality tale for all who will listen to his sermon. And those who didn't get the chance to hear it, could always buy the pamphlet:

And the condemned criminal, considering how near he is approaching the fatal hour, whenever the clock strikes – one every toll of the bell, a thrill of horror passes through him, at the prospect of disgracefully ending his days and being suddenly summoned to account – to see a prisoner in his confinement – or to feel for him in his solitary cell, which has so small an opening, as to admit one ray of the sun's light, just enough to enable him to see a part of his dark and miserable abode – to hear his bitter lamentations and witness his dreadful apprehensions is a painful sight – but one thinks lightly even of that grief, when compared to the grief to be felt bye and bye under condemnation of God's law.

Richard Tomlinson was probably the star attraction of the day, although the two scheduled to die alongside Tomlinson, Charles Shaw and Mary Smith, must have provided some added value. Charles was only 16 years old. He'd used a length of cord to strangle an even younger boy, John Holdcroft, for the princely sum of 1*s* 6*d*.

Mary Smith was sentenced to hang for infanticide. She'd drowned her 12-day-old baby in the canal at Bloxwich. According to all reports, Mary was in a state of nervous exhaustion – perhaps nowadays she would be diagnosed with post-natal depression. According to a broadside of the time, 'it was with great difficulty the learned and humane Judge could repress his feelings in passing sentence for her to die on the next Wednesday.' However, he managed to put on the black cap and condemn her nonetheless. Richard Tomlinson, the third member of the trio was described in a broadsheet published between sentence and execution as:

A rough-looking man, aged about 22 . . . tried on Monday 17th March before Mr Justice Pattison, at the Staffordshire Assizes, charged with the Wilful Murder of Mary Evans, his sweetheart, and a very interesting and amiable young woman. The trial excited much interest.

Alas, the crowd was to be mildly disappointed – a last-minute reprieve for Charles Shaw meant the spectacle would be reduced to a double bill. But still they would get to see Mary Smith, and more especially, Richard Tomlinson 'turned off'.

Tomlinson's march to the scaffold had begun several months previously in the village of Ranton, or as the *Staffordshire Advertiser* would have it: 'The secluded village of Ranton, which is distant about 6 miles from the town, from henceforth . . . distinguished as the scene of a murder, unparalleled in any of its circumstances.' On Monday 16 December 1833, a body was found in a ditch. According to the *Staffordshire Advertiser*, it was that of:

Mary Evans, daughter of Joseph Evans . . . about 20 and possessing considerable personal attraction . . . in a lifeless state, lying in a ditch, in a road, at Ranton, within 200 yards of an inhabited house and not far from the church. The body lay lengthwise in the ditch, with the face downwards, and was partially gathered up, one leg being extended and the other down under it. Her bonnet was very much crushed, and her cloak in a disordered state over her shoulders, as though she had been struggling. There was water in the ditch, its usual depth of 2½ inches increased to about 4 or 5 by the body interrupting the current. Her umbrella lay beside her in the ditch. The waggoner, having obtained assistance, the body was brought out, and was found to be warm, life having but recently become extinct. The corpse was conveyed in a cart without delay to the house of Thomas Tildesley, whose wife is the deceased's sister, and where the deceased had been living for several weeks previously, up to the time of this tragical event, and which she had left less than 24 hours before, in a state of perfect health, and in the bloom of youth and beauty.

Suspicion immediately fell on Richard Tomlinson, who was known to be courting Mary. The young couple were supposed to be walking together to her sister's house in Knightley. However, Tomlinson also had a 'reputation' – one that would not have endeared him to Joseph Evans, Mary's father.

Joseph was the parish clerk of Ranton. In those days, this would have been an esteemed position within a village community. When Richard Tomlinson came calling on his daughter Mary, one can't imagine that Evans was best pleased. Or as the *Advertiser* had it: 'the young woman whose tragical death forms the subject of our narrative, did not, we fear, possess principles of the strictest virtue, as her connection with Tomlinson would imply.'

Tomlinson had been orphaned at the age of 11, when his father and mother died in quick succession. His father's death, however, was no ordinary affair and the *Staffordshire Advertiser* (22 December 1833) was quick to pick up on this:

It is not the least remarkable circumstance of this awful case, that Tomlinson's mother died under suspicion of being a murderess. She was supposed to have poisoned her own husband. On the 1st of

November 1822, the body of her husband, John Tomlinson, of Ranton, was disinterred after being buried upwards of a week. It was opened and examined by Mr R Hughes, surgeon, who discovered arsenic in the stomach. The wretched woman was confined to her bed with the jaundice when the alleged unnatural crime was perpetrated. At the coroner's inquest, which occupied 2 whole days, we believe proof was given that she had ordered on the children to bring the basin which contained the parritch [porridge] for her husband's supper to her bedside, and that she shook something out of a paper into it. The ill-fated man was taken ill in the course of the night, and died the next day. Other suspicious circumstances were elicited, the jury returned a verdict of wilful murder, and she was committed to the county gaol for trial where,

The route taken by Richard Tomlinson and Mary Evans. The author

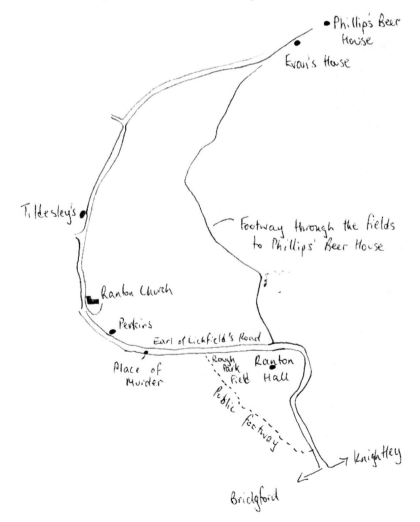

however, she died. She manifested the utmost indifference to the instruction of the chaplain, but asserted her innocence to the last.

When Mary's body was found, immediately a search party was sent to look for Richard Tomlinson. However, as the villagers were out hunting for him along the lanes of Ranton, Tomlinson was propping up the bar of a local beer shop where he also lived, which was run by his own sister. Then a local farmer called Betteley, who had not yet heard about the murder, joined him at the bar for a drink, where (according to the *Staffordshire Advertiser*) the following bizarre exchange took place:

'Did you see me do it?' 'Do what?' said Betteley; at a loss to understand his meaning. 'Murder Mary Evans,' rejoined Tomlinson. Betteley, supposing from the coolness of his manner, that he was not in earnest, told him he did not believe him; but he repeated his former assertion, saying that he had killed her, and that she was lying in a ditch under an oak tree in Mr Addison's field, not far from Perkin's.

Tomlinson was arrested by the local constable, a man by the name of Arkenstall, and taken to the lock-up at Gnosall. Here, he continued to confess freely to what he had done in front of Mr Lloyd, who was both the Vicar of Ranton and a magistrate. They took Tomlinson to a local pub called *The Horns* and here Tomlinson spilled out his confession:

'I did it. I am ready to die for it. I only wish I may be laid at her side . . . ' He said that on Sunday afternoon he had accompanied Mary Evans to her sister's at Knightley, where they remained all night. On the following morning they started for High Ercall, to consult a conjurer about some things that Mary had lost; and he being taken poorly on the road and therefore not able to travel, they returned together through Knightley on their way to Ranton. Some words occurred between them. She told him that his refusing to go to Ercall was a proof of his guilt; and she now believed he had stolen her things. He retorted that he had lost a watch and some sovereigns, and he thought she had taken them. They continued thus to criminate and recriminate each other; and amongst other charges made by him was one that the deceased had on the day before stopped on the road and talked to a waggoner of Mr Ash's, and

All Saints' Church, Ranton. Richard Tomlinson killed Mary Evans just a few yards from the spot, then later confessed to the vicar. The author

'that was not fair.' She replied, 'that had nothing to do with him.' They were both in a violent passion. And as they were coming down the road from Ranton Hall, she reproached him by saying that 'his father was poisoned and his mother died in gaol.' This exasperated him to an excessive degree, and he told her if she repeated those words he would knock her into the ditch with his fist. She did repeat them, and he knocked her into the ditch with his fist. She shouted out, 'You've murdered me.' 'Upon which [he shouted], 'If I have not, I will do it . . . [He confessed] I immediately jumped upon her back as she lay face downward in the ditch. I then stepped on the bank; and she scrambled up on her hands and knees and laid her head, with her hands on either side of it, on the ditch bank. I then left her and whether she fell into the ditch again or not I cannot say.'

The newspaper went on to cast doubt on the accuracy of elements of the confession:

From the evidence taken before the Coroner, it would appear, that his statement is not quite correct. When the body was discovered, a large rough stone, weighing at least 2 lb, was observed lying upon the right hand. A wound at the back of the deceased's head had evidently been caused by some blunt instrument applied with considerable force; and the inference is that the stone in question was used for that purpose. Tomlinson denies, we believe, having used a stone; and says that the wound must have been made by the heel of his shoe when he jumped upon the body.

According to the same newspaper article, Tomlinson, who had already been discharged from at least one regiment, and who had sold the property that he inherited on his twenty-first birthday and spent the money on drink and dissipation, showed little remorse:

Up to the time of his being delivered at the county gaol, on Wednesday, he had not betrayed the slightest emotions of distress since he perpetrated the awful deed? To the constable he talked of the matter as a person would of the most unimportant occurrence; and he requested, on Tuesday, when taken from Gnosall to Ranton, to be present at the inquest, that he might pass the place where the body was found. There he pointed out the exact spot, where he threw the victim into the ditch, without evincing the least degree of sensibility. During the inquest he sat in an adjoining room, and, although

Gnosall Lock-up. The lock-up has been re-sited from its original position after a lorry crashed into it. It was usually used for petty criminals, such as drunks and vagrants. Richard Tomlinson was taken here after confessing to the murder of Mary Evans. The author

he did not say much unless spoken to, yet, when questioned, he answered every enquiry respecting the murder with incredible indifference of manner. When brought before the Coroner and jury he was equally unmoved, and he listened to a reading of every part of the evidence, his countenance remaining unaltered the whole time. We understand that he intimated his desire to see the unfortunate young woman on Wednesday morning, before coming to gaol, and the constable complied with his wish by allowing him to call at Tildesley's and view it. Even then his obduracy was not overcome, although we are told he kissed the body, shook one of the hands, and asked for its forgiveness.

It was a short trial. The jury swiftly found Tomlinson guilty and the Judge passed sentence of death on him. According to reports Tomlinson remained impassive – even indifferent – throughout.

There was no doubt whatsoever about Richard Tomlinson's guilt. He had confessed in the pub and had been tried on strong evidence. To cap it all, he also signed a confession:

Stafford County Prison
March 18th 1834

I Richard Tomlinson, of Ranton, do upon the Word of a Dying Man, acknowledge the justice of my Sentence, and most solemnly declare that the HORRID VICES of DRUNKENNESS and SABBATH BREAKING, as well as WICKED COMPANY have brought me to the dreadful DEATH which I am now about to suffer for MURDER, and I earnestly entreat all my Fellow Creatures to remember the Words of a Dying Penitent: 'Except ye repent ye shall all likewise perish.'

Richard Tomlinson

This confession was soon copied and run off the presses of Morgan the printer, as a kind of morality tale for others who might stray from the paths of righteousness. It sold well to the crowd in front of the gaol baying for his, and Mary Smith's, blood.

CHAPTER 5

The Strangulation of Mary Malpas: a Tale of Obsessive Love 1835

The last suspicion that would have arisen was that he would perpetrate any such offence as that now attributed to him ...

Betley is a pretty little village on the Staffordshire–Cheshire border. It's the sort of village where people lead a quiet life away from the hustle and bustle of the city. It's not the setting you'd expect for a murder and that's the way it has been for some time. According to William Whites' 1834 *Gazetteer & Directory of Staffordshire*:

> *Betley is one of the smallest and pleasantest market towns in the county, consisting of one wide street, on the Nantwich road, 7½ miles W.N.W. of Newcastle-under-Lyme, near the confines of Cheshire; the boundary line between the two counties extending here through the middle of a fine lake of 80 acres, called Betley Mere, and abounding in pike perch, and other fish, some of which have been caught as heavy as 30 lb ... The appearance of the houses is uncommonly neat ... The parish contains about 1,200 acres of land, and 870 inhabitants.*

On 29 June 1835, the body of a young woman was found in a field by Ralph Latham and Simeon Davis, a servant to Mr George at Doddington Farm. Davis told the inquest into the death how he came upon the body:

> *About 5 o'clock on Monday morning ... I was going to fetch up my master's cows, and on going through Chapel Field, Hunsterston. I*

saw a woman lying on the ground, near the hedge; she was lying on her back, but inclining towards her right side; her gown and petticoats appeared much disordered; she had her bonnet on, but it was much torn in front, and her cloak was rucked up, and lay under her head as if she had been violently struggling; two clean aprons which were folded up, and her comb, lay by her side. I did not observe any marks of violence on her person; I felt at her, and found she was quite dead; I did not know her; Ralph Latham, my fellow servant, was with me; we neither of us knew her; her face was much drawn on one side, and discoloured; we supposed she was a stranger; we both knew the deceased well when she was alive, but had no idea that the woman we saw in the field was Mary Malpas; we left her where we first saw her, and returned to our master's; met several persons on the road, and told them there was a woman lying dead in Chapel Field.

The surgeon called to investigate the death was a John Twemlow from Hatherton, who described what he saw to the inquest:

I was sent for to examine the body of a woman, who was found dead in a field near Pepper-street Moss; I found her lying on her back, inclining to her right side. On examining her person, I found considerable blackness and darkness round her neck, with here and there a scratch; the discolouration on the neck seemed to have been made from violent pressure of the hand and appeared general round the throat. On examining the lower part of her body, I found a considerable degree of blackness on the inside of her thighs, and several scratches. If to violate her person had been the object of her destroyer, I have every reason to believe he did not effect his purpose. The ground round about where she lay was much disturbed, as if two persons had been violently struggling; and I am decidedly of opinion the deceased came to her death by strangulation from some person's hands.

Mr E Barker, a surgeon from Audlem, arrived at around 4 o'clock in the afternoon to examine Mary. His evidence backed up that of his colleague:

On examining the upper part of her throat I found there had been much pressure and violence on each side of her windpipe, with the appearance of fingernails penetrating through the skin, producing strangulation. On examining the thighs and legs I found much redness and discolouration about them, produced apparently from excessive friction, as though she had been struggling violently with some person. I believe her person had not been violated, but that an attempt had been made. There was also much blackness and redness about the face and on the upper part of her breasts. The discolouration of the upper part of the body is to be accounted for by the pressure on the vessels of the neck, preventing the return of the blood; consequently the minute vessels would become distended, producing blackness and swelling on the surface of the body. I am decidedly of opinion she died from strangulation.

A short time later, and not more than a mile away, John Shuker, a local labourer – knowing nothing of the tragedy that had befallen Mary – called at Mr Davison's house to fetch a man by the name of Thomas Bagguley. Another of Mr Davison's servants, 50-year-old Bagguley, had agreed to help Shuker with some calves. Despite the arrangement, Bagguley hadn't turned up for work, so Shuker then called at Bagguley's house to see where he had got to, but Mrs Bagguley told him that her husband wasn't there – in fact he had been out all night and had never returned. While they found this rather strange – Thomas Bagguley had an exemplary work record and was the caring father of eight children – Shuker decided to start his day's work and wait for his friend to turn up later. He told the inquest:

After tying up the cows I went to fetch the calves out of a hay crib adjoining the cow-house, thinking the calves might be there, though it was not the usual place they were kept in. The hasp was on the staple of the doorpost and a hanging lock through the staple, but not locked. On opening the door I observed a man's legs, the knees of which were bent, and his feet touching the straw under him. I started back alarmed; on recovering myself I went in, and taking him by the shoulders I turned his face towards me, and saw it was Thomas Bagguley. He was suspended by a rope tied round his neck with a running noose, fastened to a ladder which was over the hole where the hay is put down into the hay crib below to fodder the cows. On seeing his face, I knew it to be Thomas Bagguley, Mr Davison's labourer; he was quite dead. I alarmed Mr Davison's family, and went with two men to the hay crib, when Simeon Davis took out his knife and cut him down. It was a small cord which was round his neck.

It seemed strange that there should be two such bizarre deaths within such a short distance and time of one another in the usually quiet, agricultural village. The two deaths seemed to be connected, that much was obvious, especially as the key to the front door of the Davison's house, where Mary lived, was in Bagguley's pocket. But how had it got there and what had happened? Gossip and an inquest into both deaths attempted to piece together the story of Mary Malpas and Thomas Bagguley's last moments ....

The night before the murder Mary had asked permission to leave the Davison's house to visit her mother, who was reportedly very ill. The *Staffordshire Advertiser* reports:

On Monday morning, just after midnight, Mrs Davison was awakened by Mary MALPAS, the deceased, knocking at her door and asking if she might leave the house, as someone had brought her word that her mother was dangerously ill, and wanted her to go home directly. Mrs D did not ask her who the messenger was, but immediately gave her permission, and heard her go downstairs and out of the doors, never to return again. Mrs D soon afterwards went down to see that the door was secure, when she found it was locked, and the key gone, taken as she supposed by the young woman in order to let herself in again on her return. On Mr Davison's family rising in the morning, a ladder was found on the grass plot below the window of the girl's room; it had been brought from another part of the premises, and it is supposed for the purpose of awakening the young woman without disturbing the family.

However, Ann Malpas, Mary's mother, later swore to the inquest: 'I did not send ... anyone to my daughter to say I was ill, and if she wished to see me alive must come directly. I was not at all unwell on that day, but as well as ever I was in my life.'

According to the *Staffordshire Advertiser*, Mary's 'conduct had been most exemplary ... she is described as having been a remarkably fine girl, with pleasing manners, and of an address

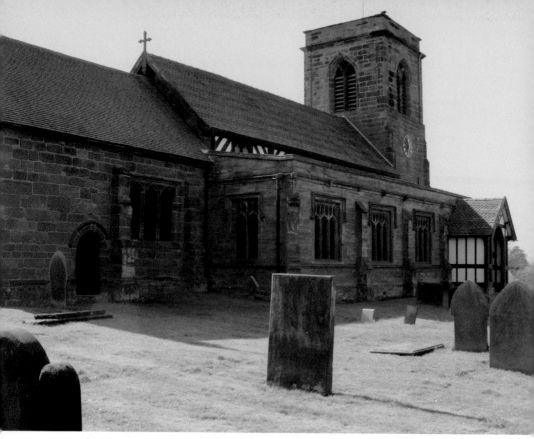

St Margaret's Church, Betley. The grave of Mary Malpas can be seen in the foreground. The author

rather superior to her situation in life.' So it is unlikely that she was lying about her mother's ill-health; it would seem reasonable to assume that someone had deliberately misled her. At the same time, at the Bagguley house, Thomas Bagguley had on several occasions refused to go up to bed. His son, also called Thomas, told the inquest that on that Sunday night:

> *My mother asked my father to go to bed several times, about 9.30; she went to bed about 10 o'clock; she requested him to go with her; he said, 'I am coming,' but did not follow her; I then locked the door, and left the key in the lock, and said, 'Father, come to bed;' he again said, 'I am coming,' but did not follow me. When I was in bed I heard my mother several times call to him to come to bed; his answer invariable was, 'I am coming;' about 2 o'clock my mother awoke, and not finding him in bed she went downstairs; he was not in the house; the door was locked and the key put under the door. I got up about 4 o'clock, and found the door locked, and the key put*

under; when I went to bed I locked the door and left the key in the lock.

According to the *Staffordshire Advertiser*:

Bagguley had previously been employed for 21 years by Mr Richard Dobson, and had the character of a quiet, honest, hard-working man: he was of rather a reserved disposition, and not given to conversation, He was about 50 years of age and had a wife and a family of eight children living. From his conduct for a number of years, the last suspicion that would have arisen was that he would perpetrate any such offence as that now attributed to him, nor is it known that the slightest intimacy existed between him and the young woman.

However, the inquest into the two deaths couldn't fail to find a link between them. The inquest's verdict on Thomas Bagguley was 'That the deceased feloniously and wilfully destroyed himself by suspending himself to a ladder, with a small cord, on the morning of the 29th June.' They also decided that Mary's death was one of 'Wilful murder against Thomas Bagguley, deceased, for having in the night of Sunday, June 28th, feloniously and wilfully destroyed the deceased Mary Malpas, by strangulation.'

The reporter from the *Staffordshire Advertiser* put the details of the two deaths together, emphasising the fact that Bagguley wouldn't go to bed and that he had the Davison's door-key in his pocket, and decided that:

Bagguley was the man who inveigled the girl from the house under the false pretence of her mother's illness, and in the sequel perpetrated the awful crime of murder. Our readers will draw their own conclusion from the evidence given at the inquest, and now laid before them.

The opinion formed by those who reside upon the spot, and are best acquainted with the circumstances is, that the wretched man's contrivance of decoying the ill-fated girl from her master's house in the dead of night, was only with the intention of gratifying a lust which, under all the circumstances, cannot be attributed to anything less than Satanic influence; and then finding the unfortunate object of his desires virtuous to death, and fearing his iniquitous conduct would come to light, deprived his hapless victim of her life! Supposing this view to be correct, it is easy to imagine, that stung with remorse and goaded by the same fiend-like spirit, the wretched man decided to finish the tragical occurrence by a suicidal act.

Had the two arranged to meet? Or had Bagguley trapped Mary into meeting him on a pretext? If they had agreed to meet, given the lateness of the hour, then surely it must have been for some kind of tryst, then perhaps matters simply got out of hand. However, the huge gap in their ages might indicate otherwise. It would be unlikely that Mary would be dallying with someone of Bagguley's age, especially given the fact that there were obviously plenty of young men nearer her own age around.

The newspaper report seems as good an explanation as any: Bagguley had become infatuated with the pretty young girl and, when she wouldn't succumb to his wishes, killed her. Unable to live with what he had done, he then killed himself. Of course, there has to be an element of conjecture in all this. We will never know the whole story of what happened to Mary Malpas and Thomas Bagguley on that summer's night, in the normally tranquil village of Betley.

Grave of Mary Malpas, St Margaret's Church, Betley. The author

CHAPTER 6

Christina Collins and the Bloody Steps
1839

*I heard a noise at the lock – a cry,
I thought as if somebody was
abusing a child – a cry of distress ...*

In the early hours of the morning of 16 June 1839, Thomas Grant, a boatman on the Trent & Mersey Canal, was approaching Brindley Bank near Rugeley, when he saw something strange floating on the water. From his side of the canal, it looked like a bundle of clothes, but for some reason his suspicions were aroused. He hooked the bundle and dragged it to the towpath. It was immediately obvious that it was the body of a young woman. She was still warm and, with her black and swollen face, it looked as though she had been strangled. With the help of John Johnson, a passer-by, he hauled the body out of the water and the two men carried the body to the *Talbot Inn* in Rugeley. The Police were sent for. From the information they were given, they stopped a boat further down the canal at Fazeley.

The murdered woman was Christina Collins. At 37 she was still a trim figure and had, for the times, led an exciting life. Her family had once been prosperous – her father made machines for the Nottingham lace-making industry – but he failed to capitalise on early success and died in poverty. Christina's first marriage had been to a man called Thomas Ingleby, who styled himself, 'The Emperor of all the Conjurors'. Ingleby was the author of a book entitled, *The Whole Art of Legerdemain*. He also performed sleight of hand tricks, including one rather unpleasant one, in which he would decapitate a live chicken, hold up the bloody head for all to see, and then apparently revive the dead animal – actually substituting it with a second, live chicken. Christina soon became his assistant, presumably part of her role being to procure yet more live chickens.

Ingleby died in 1832. He was several years older than Christina, who was only 30 at the time. It was natural enough that she should remarry and in 1838 she met Robert Collins. While Christina found work as a seamstress in Liverpool, Robert had less joy and, as many have done before and many will do again, he went off to London to find work. Wanting his new wife to join him as soon as possible, he sent her a guinea to pay for her passage. Travel by rail or stagecoach would have been too expensive, so Christina Collins paid 16 shillings from her guinea for the fare to London by canal boat.

The boat she travelled on belonged to Pickford & Co. Its captain was a man called James Owen and his crew consisted of two men, William Ellis and George Thomas, and a young lad called William Musson. Many of those who worked the canal boats in those days were men who went under assumed names because of criminal pasts, so there were several alibis in use. It

The Shrew, *Rugeley. Formerly known as the* Talbot Arms, *it figures twice in this book. It was here that the body of Christina Collins was brought after being found in the canal. Room 10 was where John Parsons Cook died of poisoning at the hands of William Palmer.* The author

was all four of them who were arrested for the rape and murder of Christina Collins. However, even before the trial began, William Musson was released without charge, as he was deemed too young to have any involvement.

Mr Justice Williams ruled early on in the case that there was not enough evidence to proceed with the charge of rape, which was dropped. However, he did accede to the prosecution's request to delay the trial. They had another potential witness, a man who had been James Owen's cellmate in Stafford Gaol, and they wanted to approach him as a witness.

James Owen's cellmate was a man by the name of James Orgill. He told the court that while Owen had shared a cell with him, Owen had insisted that it was the other two men, Ellis and Thomas, who had committed the murder, and that he'd been fast asleep at the time. In fact, he later swore that:

> *Being drunk with the whisky or one thing and another I was very loathe to get up, but I did get up. The boy went to drive the horse; I steered the boat. The other two were in the cabin with the woman. They got the bottle to have some more whisky and while they were having it the woman slipped out of the cabin into the hatches where I was. She made an attempt to get out of the boat and got her legs halfway into the water. I leaned over and pulled her out. They pulled her into the cabin again where they committed rapes upon her to death.*

Owen's statement made no impression and Orgill's evidence carried little weight. That of William Musson, the boat's boy must have carried slightly more. He stated clearly that he'd heard Ellis snoring at the time the murder was supposed to have taken place. Perhaps it was Musson's statement that helped to save Ellis's life.

Throughout the trial as each witness was called in turn, it became evident that Pickford's boatmen, fuelled by the liquor they were stealing from casks that were part of their cargo, had been mistreating Christina all long the canal. There were plenty of witnesses to the way in which Christina had been treated by the boatmen during her short trip from Preston Brook, where she had joined the vessel. As each witness took the stand, the circumstantial case against the boatmen became stronger.

Canal Lock, Stone. Christina Collins complained to a clerk of the Trent & Mersey Canal Company about her treatment here. The author

At Stoke-on-Trent, Christina Collins complained to a Pickford's porter, William Brookes. Brookes also testified that he heard her say to Thomas, 'Leave me alone, I'll have nothing to say to you,' and told the court that the crew was drunk. His wife accompanied Christina Collins for a few miles on board the barge in order to keep an eye on the poor woman, who was obviously increasingly the target of the crew's lascivious thoughts as they grew more and more drunk.

By Stone, she was complaining to Hugh Cordwell, cheque clerk to the Trent & Mersey Canal Company, who also saw that the boatmen were all intoxicated and noted that James Owen, the Captain, was particularly drunk. He told her that she should report her worries when she got to the end of her journey.

Just outside Stone, at Aston Lock, the assistant clerk John Tansley saw her walking on the towpath before she rejoined the boat. It would not have been unusual for a passenger to walk alongside a boat from time-to-time, especially given the canal barges moved at around 3 miles an hour, so although Tansley heard one of the crew shouting abuse at her, he thought little of it at the time.

By 9 o'clock and in the same area, Thomas Bloor, Captain of a boat named *The Emerald* passed them. He had a drink with

Milepost on the Trent & Mersey Canal. Christine Collins was last seen alive not far from here. The author

them and testified later that the men were all pretty drunk. Bloor stated that Owen was crude about what he'd do to his lady passenger. Owen is also supposed to have said that he would 'burke' his passenger, which was taken as a reference to William Burke of 'Burke and Hare' fame – the Edinburgh body snatchers, who, when they ran out of newly buried bodies to sell for dissection, killed fresh ones of their own.

Another boat's captain, Robert Walker also saw a woman walking along the towpath. Shortly after, he too saw the Pickford's boat and one of the crew asked him if he'd seen a woman. He also explained that one of the boatmen had used foul language about Christina, describing what the crew would like to do to her once they caught up with her.

At Shirleywich, the lock-keeper's wife, Anne Mills, was woken up by Christina's screams:

I heard a noise at the lock – a cry, I thought as if somebody was abusing a child – a cry of distress. I got up and opened the window. A boat of Pickford's was in the lock. I knew it was Pickford's boat by the letter board. They are large white letters different to any of the other boats . . . I saw a woman at the top of the cabin . . . with her legs hanging on the outside. There were three men – in the boat.

'Don't attempt me. I'll not go down,' she cried 'I'll not go in there.'

'What woman is that with you?' I called to the man under the window.

'A passenger.'

'Is there anybody with her?'

'Her husband.'

At Woodend Lock, near King's Bromley, Owen went to Anne Sleigh, wife of Jonathan Sleigh, lock-keeper at Woodend Lock and told her a woman had drowned.

'I am afraid she is; I cannot think what has become of her; she appeared to be deranged; she had got into the canal once up to her knees, and I pulled her out, and took her into the cabin.

However, the three men and the boy hadn't reported the loss of their passenger at Rugeley, which is where the body was found. They were consequently arrested a few miles further down the canal and swiftly brought before Staffordshire Assizes.

The *Staffordshire Advertiser* reported the entire trial and the reporter was obviously most impressed with the Judge's summing up and his

. . . remarking in a lucid manner upon the more particular points. He observed that he never met with a case which had a larger demand upon his patience, attention and discrimination. His Lordship alluded to the observation made by Mr Godson [for the defence] respecting the minds of the jury being almost naturally prejudiced against the prisoners, remarking that though the benefits arising from a free press were inestimable they [the jury] must dismiss from their minds anything they had either heard or read; to apply their minds to the evidence, and to the evidence alone. The charge against the three prisoners was the murder of Christina Collins and effecting that murder by drowning. Before they found all or any of them guilty, they must be satisfied that they did drown her: That they effected her death in this way, and in no other way. The learned Judge after pointing out the contradictory statements of some of the witnesses, alluded to the evidence of Orgill, observing

that his testimony must be received with great caution, for he was a tainted witness. The statement of Owen, being made in the absence of other prisoners, did not affect them at all. His Lordship next adverted to the evidence of Mr Barnett, the surgeon who had examined the body, whose opinion was, that the woman had died from suffocation produced by drowning. He implored them to consider the case attentively and minutely, to satisfy their minds before returning a verdict, that the deceased woman came to her death in the particular way described in the indictment; and whether it was the act of the prisoners conjointly, or two of them, or any single one. The conviction of prisoners was not the first object in an English court of justice. However, desirable it was that the guilty should not escape punishment, it was far better for the guilty man to escape than for the innocent man to suffer, the learned Judge, in concluding implored the jury not to allow any feelings of disgust or prejudice they might entertain, either to have any weight in their verdict, or induce them to relax in a minute enquiry into all the facts which had been brought before them . . . .

The customary proclamation for silence having been made, and the learned Judge having put on his coif, addressed the prisoners in the following terms, in a very impressive and solemn manner, the most deadly silence prevailing, and the prisoners still continuing unmoved: 'You, James Owen, George Thomas and William Ellis,

Christina Collins' last journey – the stretch of the Trent & Mersey Canal from Stoke to Fradley Junction. The author

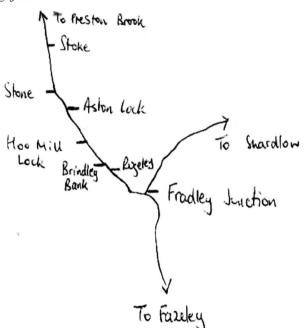

The Trent & Mersey Canal at Brindley Bank. It was here that Thomas Grant pulled Christina Collins form the canal. The author

after a long and patient hearing of your case, after mature delibera-tion, a jury of your country have felt themselves constrained to find you guilty of a foul murder – a murder committed upon an unoffending woman who was placed under your protection, who, there is too much reason to fear, was first the object of your lusts, and then, to prevent detection of that crime, the object of your violence. Look not for pardon in this world. Apply to God, of mercy for that pardon which he extends to all penitent sinners. Prepare yourselves for the ignominious death which awaits you. The case is a most painful and a most disgusting one. It only remains for me to pass upon you the awful sentence of the law, which is, that you be taken hence to the place from whence you came, from thence to the place of execution, and that you and each of you be hanged by the neck until you are dead, that your bodies be afterwards buried within the precincts of the County prison and may the Lord have mercy on you.'

The learned Judge was much affected in passing the sentence, and at the conclusion shed tears.

The prisoners heard the sentence utterly unmoved, and left the bar with perfect indifference – Ellis smiling as he went down the stairs, but the countenance of Owen slightly changed.

Perhaps Ellis was smiling because he thought he wouldn't hang. As it was, during their wait, an appeal was lodged on his behalf, arguing that he should be treated with leniency as he was less involved in the crime than Owen and Thomas.

On 11 April 1840, as the three men were being given their final holy communion by the prison chaplain, Ellis heard that the appeal had been successful and his sentence was commuted to that of deportation to Australia for 14 years. Why the prison authorities left it so late, one cannot tell, because news of the commutation of his sentence had reached the prison during the previous night. It may have been inefficiency on their part, or possibly some kind of sadistic trick – leave Ellis to think he would hang until the last possible moment and taunt the other two with Ellis's reprieve from the death sentence: these were cruel times.

So it was that only Owen and Thomas made the long walk to the scaffold. Reports indicate that as many as 10,000 people turned up to watch the event. Hangings were a popular spectator sport throughout the country and you could always expect a good crowd in Stafford. William Calcraft was the executioner. His assistant for the day, whose job often included throwing himself at the legs of the dangling prisoners to ensure their necks were broken, was a man by the name of Cheshire, often referred to by the nickname 'Old Cheese'. Cheshire stopped off at an inn on his way to the gaol, where he became so drunk that he never arrived to play his part in the execution of the boatmen.

Calcraft needed a temporary assistant and found one in the shape of George Smith, who was detained in the gaol for a debt, which he managed to work off by acting as Calcraft's assistant for the day. Not only did this work get Smith out of gaol, but it also proved to be a vocation for him, as he was soon hanging people in his own right, acquiring the nickname of 'The Dudley Higgler'. He was the man who would later put the noose around William Palmer's neck, in one of the highest-profile hangings of the era (see Chapter 11).

While the circumstantial evidence against Owen, Ellis and Thomas was enough to convict them at the time, there have always been certain doubts about the case, as some of the

The Grave of Christine Collins is in the same churchyard, St Augustine's Rugeley, as John Parsons Cook, for whose murder Palmer hanged. The inscription on the grave reads: 'To the memory of Christina Collins, wife of Robert Collins, London, who having been most barbarously treated was found dead in the canal in this parish on June 17th 1839 aged 37 years.' This stone is erected by some individuals of the parish of Rugeley in commemoration of the end of the unhappy woman. The author evidence was contradictory. Indeed, in his book *The Wench is Dead*, Colin Dexter's detective Morse, while hospitalised, revisits a fictionalised version of the case and decides that the whole business is an elaborate insurance scam.

Unfortunately, whatever the verdict of the case, the outcome for poor Christina Collins was still the same. She was buried in Rugeley churchyard, where her tomb remains to this day, local people having subscribed to buy her a decent headstone.

In the tradition of the day, as Owen and Thomas swung, ballad sellers were out peddling their wares. Under the headline of 'The Lives Trial & Execution of Pickford's Two Boatmen' came the following doggerel:

Good Christian people pray attend
While I relate to you,
Concerning of a murder foul,
It is, alas! too true.
A helpless female much beloved,
Was travelling to her home.
Three boatmen seized her as she sat,
The water was her home.
A letter she had just received,
From her beloved friend,
It was her husband you shall hear,
That did for her then send.
Upon the water she did go,
It was the nearest way
But sad to tell she never more,
Did see the light of day.
James Owen soon did her affright,
The wretched woman cry'd
Dobel [One of the gang's aliases] *he said 'tis all in vain,*
All help it is deny'd.
Ellis he then assisted them,
They bruised her body sore,
Their hearts did never once relent,
Till life it was no more.
It was on the 17th day of June,
This murder it was done,

Not the original Bloody Steps of Christina Collins fame, but their replacement – a new flight of concrete steps leading up from the Trent & Mersey canal at Brindley Bank. The author

They did complete the awful deed,
Before the rising sun.
Loud was her shrieks, but all was vain,
She all her strength did try,
To save her life she struggled long,
But now she was to die.
Her voice grew faint, life's ebbing stream
Did flow upon the boat,
The glassy eye convinced them all,
That they the deed had wrought.
They threw the body overboard
To hide the crime they'd done,
But Providence did so ordain,
The body should be found.
In Staffordshire these monsters was,
In Rugeley you shall hear.
They now in prison lie condemn'd
Their sentence is past here.

CHAPTER 7

The Cost of Living
1843

The crime ... was one of the most cold-blooded and heartless murders that ever blackened the criminals annals of any country.

Executions were always popular. Even serious newspapers like *The Times* enjoyed filling their columns with salacious details of the latest events. They didn't just report on them retrospectively. In the same way as there is nowadays a great deal of coverage leading up to major sporting events, such as an international football match, *The Times* (and other papers) would let its readers know when there was a good meaty hanging in the offing.

On 23 August 1843, the newspaper foreshadowed one up-coming execution with the following pre-match analysis, which had originally also appeared in a Staffordshire newspaper:

THE CONDEMENED CULPRIT CHARLES HIGGINSON. The execution of this man, now lying under sentence of death in our county prison, for the horrible murder of his child by burying him alive, will take place on Saturday morning next, the 26th inst. Higginson, for several days after his condemnation was in a very hardened and incorrigible state of mind; but the Rev. R Buckeridge, the chaplain, has succeeded at length in making some impression upon him. He now acknowledges the justice of his sentence and is sensible of his awful condition. Although a man of obtuse intellect, he appears to have received a tolerably good plain education. He can read well and can refer to any passage of Scripture in a moment.

Of course, with there being plenty of murders to choose from throughout the length and breadth of the country, and execution being relatively commonplace, crimes had to be particularly gruesome or unusual to gain more than a column-inch in the national press. While most child murder victims die at the hands of relatives, the way in which the Higginson child had died was particularly strange and unpleasant. According to *The Times*, which misspelled the names of those involved:

> *The murdered boy, who was 5 years old, was sent by his father to a nurse, named Sarah Breese, at Whitley Heath and he was to pay 1s 6d a week for his keep. Higgonson [sic] having been 11 weeks in arrears, Breese informed him that if he could not pay up the amount, he was to remove his child.*
>
> *In the course of the week he transmitted 7 weeks' payment, and the nurse, being disappointed in not receiving the whole amount, insisted upon his taking the boy with him. On the morning of the 2nd April last, Higgonson took his child away, saying, that he had got a nurse for him near his mother's house at Eccleshall. The poor child was never seen afterwards . . . .*

Friends and neighbours naturally wanted to know what had become of the child. Charles Higginson's reply was that because the child had very bad eyes, it had died on the road. So where was the body? Higginson had an answer to that too. Not having the money to pay for a proper funeral, he had buried the boy's body near the road, in some woods.

Higginson's story raised more questions than it answered. How could a child have died of poor eyesight? Why no funeral? Surely, even the poor stood some kind of chance of finding charity or friends to help pay for one? What's more, Higginson had even borrowed a spade before setting off to fetch the boy from Sarah Breese's house. Suspicions were naturally aroused and the authorities asked Higginson to take them to the place where the body was buried.

The child's makeshift grave was in Bishop's Wood. It didn't take much to reveal the little body buried beneath a few clods of soil, less than a foot below the surface. However, when the boy's body was disinterred, onlookers were shocked to see that the child's eyes and mouth had been bandaged. Higginson was unable to explain this away. The only plausible explanation was that he had killed the boy.

The Judge opened the trial by asking Higginson how he pleaded:

He replied, 'I am guilty, and beg for mercy. If you please.'

Judge – Prisoner listens – 'If you plead guilty I must pass sentence upon you, and you will be hanged.'

Prisoner – on the question being repeated, he said, after a pause, 'I am guilty, for what I did I did for want.'

Judge – 'I can take no special plea, if you persist in pleading guilty, you must take the consequence.'

From the various witness statements that were to follow, it became obvious that Charles Higginson had been the last person to see his son alive. Furthermore, there were inconsistencies in his story as to where and when the events had occurred. In one version of his story the boy had died 3 weeks before; in another he had died the previous week. In one version, Higginson's nephew had brought the news in person from Wednesbury; in another he had received a letter telling him about it. His sister-in-law, Maria Higginson, testified that:

On the 3rd April, the prisoner came to their home about dinner time. He came by himself, and she asked him how the child was. He said it was dead. She asked him when it died, to which he replied that it died on Tuesday and was buried on Thursday. She asked him what had been the matter with it, and he said it had a bad eye. She said she never knew anybody die of a bad eye, on which he observed it had been a long time of inflammation and mortification had taken place. She asked him if he often went to see the child, and whether the child cried when he left. He replied, no. The prisoner gave her two frocks, a cap and two pinafores which had belonged to the child. She gave them to the constable.

There could have been little doubt in the minds of anyone in the court that Higginson was spinning one hasty lie after another in order to protect himself. It's hardly surprising, as the details were not pleasant. The court report from Mr Greatrex, a surgeon from Eccleshall, showed that:

The child was apparently about 5 years old. He [Greatrex] examined the body, which was not much decomposed. He found a severe contusion on the right side of the head, but he observed no other external marks. He made an examination of the skull, but before doing so he had the body washed; there was a bandage over the eye, and another over the mouth tied very tightly, which produced considerable indentation of the muscles of the face. On removing the scalp, there was a bruise corresponding with the external injury, also a fracture of one of the small bones behind the eye, the bruise was calculated to destroy life, and they appear to have been inflicted by some blunt instrument, a spade would have produced such injuries.

The Judge remarked it had been passed on to him that Higginson was of low intellect, and asked if he wanted anyone to speak on his behalf. What good it might have done, one can never be sure, but Higginson passed up the offer. Nonetheless, several people involved in the trial did step forward:

Thomas Jenkinson, an officer of the county prison stated that he had known the prisoner from his childhood; they were schoolfellows, and in those days he was never thought to have the faculties of other boys . . ..

Thomas Harris, wardsman of the county gaol, knew the prisoner when at school and spoke to the same fact . . ..

Mr Robert Hughes, surgeon to the county prison, had frequently seen the prisoner during his confinement, he was of the opinion that he was of weak intellect, but not so weak as not to know right from wrong. On cross-examination he remarked that he thought the prisoner was aware of the effect of his violence upon his child. He had not heard the trial, but in his opinion the prisoner, when he committed the act had a consciousness of what he was doing.

It took the jury just 1 minute to find Charles Higginson guilty of murder. Wearing the black coif that indicated Higginson was to hang, the Judge summed up:

Charles Higginson you have been found guilty of murder – of taking away the life of your own child, and certainly from what appears, with very little motive for so dreadful an act. Your object seems to have been to save yourself from some little expense and inconvenience to which you had been put in its maintenance. Your act appears to have been one of the most deliberate determination that can be conceived; for when you borrowed the spade early in the morning you must have contemplated your purpose. You appear to have taken this innocent child where you had prepared its grave, and having knocked him on the head you then covered him up and finished the work by suffocation. You knew what you were about when you destroyed your child, and therefore nothing is so absurd as to say you were insane, and not conscious of what you were doing. I can hold out no hope in your case. You can expect no mercy in this world. You will be attended in gaol, and I hope that you will make a proper use of the instructions which you will receive from those who are appointed to attend upon you, which is the only thing of importance in your circumstances.

None of the evidence supporting his 'weak intellect' proved that Higginson was insane. He obviously knew right from wrong: his attempts to cover up his crime are proof of this. But at the same time, he was unbelievably inept, and he had chosen the most bizarre reason for the boy's death – an eye infection. In all the reports, there are no other stories concerning Higginson's cruelty – this seems to be the only act of violence he ever committed.

The suspicion must be that the murder was Higginson's way of dealing with a problem. He drifted from one menial job to another with periods of enforced idleness in between his few days' work. He didn't have enough money to feed the child, so the child had to go – it solved his problem. While he knew this was wrong, he was intellectually incapable of seeing just *how* wrong it was. If he did have the intellectual difficulties ascribed to him, he probably had little idea of what was going on around him. Whatever Higginson's true motives, his side of the story would never have been fully heard in the courtroom; he had no lawyer to help him put forward his case.

The Times of 29 August 1843 was more severe, finding nothing to mitigate the terrible crime Higginson had committed:

It was evident, therefore, that the unnatural parent, to rid himself of his offspring's maintenance, enticed his innocent victim into the wood, where after digging a grave, having previously blindfolded him and tied a handkerchief over his mouth so as to prevent his being heard, he actually buried him alive. After his condemnation he sunk into a morbid state of insensibility, from which the un-wearied exhortations of the Rev. R Buckridge, chaplain of the county prison, were not able to rouse him. Latterly, however, he evinced a slight degree of compunction and uneasiness, and the rev. gentleman availed himself of the favourable change, in order to lay before him the importance of his awful condition. On Thursday last his father and three brothers visited him for the last time, and although the wretched culprit was not very communicative with them, yet he afterwards appeared deeply affected at the interview, and endured the deepest agony.

Higginson's actual execution was reported in the following way:

This wretched man, who was convicted at the late assize for the brutal murder of his child, was executed at Stafford on Saturday morning at 8 o'clock in front of the county gaol, in the presence of an immense concourse of persons. The crime for which the unhappy wretch forfeited his life was one of the most cold-blooded and heartless murders that ever blackened the criminals annals of any country.

On Friday the condemned sermon was preached by the rev. chaplain and the sacrament was afterwards administered to him. The scene was one of deep solemnity, and produced a most awful effect on the prisoners. The unhappy culprit passed a very restless night, and at an early hour arose, and was soon attended by the rev. ordinary of the prison, who remained with him until the last moment in deep prayer. By 7.30, all the authorities having arrived, they proceeded to the condemned cell, where the painful ceremony of pinioning the arms was gone through. He appeared perfectly calm and resigned to this fate. He approached and ascended the drop with a firm step, and bade adieu to the governor, Mr Brutton [The Times has his name as Burton], in a very affectionate manner, at the same time shedding tears.

The awful moment had now arrived: he stood while the rope was adjusted and the cap drawn over his face with remarkable fortitude, evidently in deep and fervent prayer. After the lapse of a few seconds the platform fell, and the unhappy wretch ceased to exist. The crowd did not manifest the least feeling during the ceremony, and con-ducted themselves throughout with the greatest propriety. The body, after hanging one hour, was cut down and buried within the walls of the gaol.

That the crowd could 'conduct themselves with the greatest propriety' is remarkable. Higginson must have aroused a strong level of blood-lust amongst the local population, probably less for the fact that he had killed his child – more for the way in which he had done it. For this was an age plagued by the genuine fear of being buried before one's time, and there was much talk of the insides of coffin lids being scratched by frantic occupants not yet dead. It was also an age when graveyards were haunted by 'Resurrection Men', who risked their liberty retrieving corpses and selling them on to surgeons for dissection, in what was perhaps the blackest of black markets. For at that time, only the cadavers of executed criminals could be legally dismembered: thus the principle of supply and demand made body-snatching a lucrative business. The men who did it were despised by the public (but with a suitable frisson of horror). For instance, the hanging of two murderous body-snatchers in London, in 1831, elicited the following enthusiastic report from the *Newgate Calendar*:

> *Bishop and Williams were executed outside Newgate in the presence of 30,000 spectators, who set up a shout of exultation that was prolonged for several minutes. The bodies were removed the same night, Bishop to the King's College, and Williams to the Theatre of Anatomy, in Windmill Street, Haymarket, to be dissected. They were publicly exhibited on Tuesday and Wednesday, at both places, when immense crowds of persons were admitted to see their remains.*

As a result of the crimes of Bishop and Williams and others (most notoriously Burke and Hare in Edinburgh), the Anatomy Act of 1832 was passed. This allowed anatomists to dissect the dead bodies of anyone who had been reliant on the State. This essentially meant that the bodies of the poor, who had died in workhouses, were the only ones available for medical study. But even if the law had removed all restrictions on dissection, the public's attitude to what seemed like desecration did not. In the nineteenth century, there was still a great deal of resistance to

Stafford Gaol today. The original gaol was situated a few hundred yards away. Many of the criminals featured here passed through Stafford gaol, several were hanged outside it and some buried within its walls. The author

the work of anatomists, and bodies were perhaps not as easily come by as doctors might have hoped. Mingled with the very thought that the Higginson boy had been left to suffocate in his grave, this must have caused the strongest of public reactions.

As it was, Charles Higginson, newly chastened by his readings of the Scripture, made the final walk to the scaffold. He probably had little idea of what he had done and what was about to happen to him. Given his level of intelligence and understanding, it might be fair to assume that the authorities were hanging a man whose mind worked in no more sophisticated manner than that of an 8-year-old child.

CHAPTER 8

Sarah Westwood and the Poisoned Porridge
1843

Murder perpetrated by the foulest means ...

In November 1843, Sarah Westwood decided she had had enough of her nail-maker husband, John, and slipped arsenic into his food. She might have got away with the murder had it not been for the fact that so many members of her family were happy to testify against her.

The Westwoods lived at Burntwood, near Lichfield. They had eight children, including an illegitimate child of Sarah's born before the Westwoods were married. Their domestic circumstances were described by the prosecuting counsel, Mr Corbett, in the court case against Sarah on 28 December 1843 in the following terms:

> *Unhappily, the deceased and the prisoner had lived on bad terms, originally in consequence of an attachment on the part of the prisoner to a person of the name of Samuel Phillips the conduct between [Phillips] and the prisoner had frequently been the cause of domestic strife, sometimes even proceeding to acts of violence.*

Samuel Phillips was the Westwoods' lodger and several people had witnessed rows and even violence that had arisen out of this bizarre *ménage à trois*. Mary Westwood, one of the older daughters, who no longer lived at home, told the court that she had seen her parents arguing about Phillips on several occasions. Robert Westwood, John's brother, who lived in Burntwood, told the court of several incidents where he had seen the couple arguing about her relationship with Phillips:

I don't think that the prisoner and her husband lived on good terms. I was present when they had words on the 19th October; they were to consequence of Phillips and the prisoner, having been out together the night before ... My brother asked her if she would go to a tea drinking at the Ball Inn *at Burntwood. She said no she would not. He said to her, 'If I had not wanted you to have gone you would have been there.' He said, 'Recollect you wanted to make a child of me last night by locking the door.' She said she did not, he said she did, and he told her that if she did not know better then he would teach her better ... They also had a dispute sometime in August about some ale being carried out to his house by Samuel Phillips and the prisoner ....*

William Dawson, a neighbour also, told the court:

On the 2nd September I was present at a quarrel between John Westwood and his wife and Phillips, in the road at Burntwood. Westwood said, 'D*** your eyes, what was you doing at her when I knocked you down?' I don't know whether Phillips and the prisoner had been standing together. The prisoner said, 'D*** your eyes, kill him.' Westwood got up from the ground and went at her asking, 'what were you at when I knocked Phillips down?' she said, 'D*** your eyes, I have catched ye, I came last night but I could not drop on you.' She said she would go and beg her bread from door to door before she would live with him – she had one child and would take the child with her. She went and told her little daughter to put on her bonnet and shawl and go with her. She then went away with the little girl. I did not remain there. When I first saw Phillips he was down on the ground, and Westwood was on him.

So, if Sarah Westwood had the motive to kill her husband – she obviously preferred the lodger – did she have the opportunity to carry out the deed?

The day that John Westwood died, he and Sarah, one of the older boys, Charles, and three of the youngest daughters sat down to eat lunch. As Charles Westwood told the court:

My father had gruel that day, and ... also had a little meat and bread after the gruel. I remained out of the house about an hour, and came back about 1 o'clock, when I found that my father was upstairs lying down. I did not then go upstairs, but went up to him about 5 o'clock, when I asked him whether he was going to get up and come to work again. He said he should get up again soon as he felt warm, but he then felt very chilly . . . I went up to him again soon after 9.00, and then he was dying . . . about 10 minutes after, I saw him dead. I followed my mother up to the room when I went up at 9 o'clock, and she came downstairs with me when I left; she said that my father was dead. Some of the neighbours wanted to send for the doctor, and others said it was no use. There is a surgeon living about three-quarters of a mile from our house. About 3 o'clock in the afternoon I saw my mother bring down in the chamber pot some stuff which she said my father had thrown up, and which she threw away in the soak-hole.

It seemed likely then, that if Sarah Westwood had poisoned her husband, the arsenic must have been in something that John had eaten at lunch. She was disposing of the evidence.

Eliza Westwood, the 10-year-old daughter backed up her older brother's story and went on to add that her father asked her mother, 'what that white stuff was that was in the gruel; she said she did not know. I saw no white stuff in the gruel which I had. I don't know what my mother had for dinner.'

It took John Westwood 9 hours to die. Mary Dawson, a neighbour, testified:

I saw the deceased between 11.00 and 12 o'clock at work in his shop on the day that he died. He appeared to be in very good health for anything that I know to the contrary. I went into the house between 8.00 and 9 o'clock in the evening, and went upstairs into a room over the kitchen. I took a light with me. John Westwood, the deceased, was then in the room in a dying state on the bed. The bedclothes were on the bed, but they did not cover him; he had on his stockings, drawers, waistcoat, and shirt. I did not speak to him nor he to me. I stopped in the room between 30 minutes and 1 hour, he was dead when I left the room.

Once her husband was dead, Sarah Westwood seemed most anxious to get together the correct paperwork to be able to bury him. However, the coroner decided that the circumstances of the death demanded a post-mortem, which was carried out by

Mr Charles Chavasac, a surgeon from Lichfield. He later told the court:

> *On making the post-mortem examination I found that the body was in a perfectly healthy state, but I found that the bowels were in an intense state of inflammation, the lungs were of a dark colour and were turgid, and from the general appearance of the body I suspected that there was arsenic in it. The internal organs were in a perfectly healthy state. I took out the contents of the stomach and analysed them the same day. I am perfectly acquainted with the chemical tests to ascertain the presence of arsenic. I applied a great number of them and every one of them indicated the presence of arsenic. I detected very small grains of white arsenic in the bowels . . . there was a ¼ ounce in the stomach . . . [perhaps] as much as ½ ounce. The effects of such a quantity would . . . be seen in an hour after it was taken . . . it would produce a sleepy, drowsy sensation and chilliness. The cause of the deceased's death was from arsenic.*

So, if she had both opportunity and motive, and seemed to want her husband buried with almost indecent haste, did she in fact possess any arsenic with which to carry out the deed?

When Mary Westwood had visited her mother in gaol while awaiting trial, she asked her mother:

> *Where she was on the 1st November. She told me she was in Walsall to buy some poison. I asked her what she bought it for. She said that she and my father had some breaking out on their bodies and Hannah Mason [Samuel Phillips's mother] told her that poison would cure it.*

John Raymond, Inspector of Police at Shenstone also testified that as he was escorting Sarah Westwood to gaol:

She said she was with Hannah Moore, and that she had made some purchases in two or three shops in Walsall for her daughter. I asked her whether she had been to a chemist's shop; she said she had not, and that she had never purchased a bit of poison in her life.

This contradiction in the two pieces of evidence was crucial. If Sarah Westwood had bought arsenic – which of course was far more commonly used than it is today – why did she suddenly deny having done so? The case seemed straightforward enough.

Sarah Westwood's defence lawyer attempted to show that there was no direct evidence linking Sarah with the death, but the jury was to think otherwise. As the *Staffordshire Advertiser* reported:

The jury then consulted together for about 15 minutes, when the foreman delivered their verdict: 'guilty; but we recommend her to mercy, my Lord.'

The Judge: 'On what grounds gentlemen?'

The jury did not immediately answer; but on the Judge remarking that he must ask them on what grounds they made the recommendation, the foreman replied, 'We wish to recommend her to your mercy, my Lord, that is all.'

The Judge: 'On no other ground?

The Foreman: 'No, my Lord.'

His Lordship, in reply to Mr Yardley, said he should direct a general verdict of guilty on all the counts of the indictment.

The prisoner who, throughout the trial had been seated in the dock, apparently absorbed in grief, on hearing the verdict burst forth into piteous cries, saying, that she was as innocent as a child unborn ...

The learned Judge passed sentence as follows: Sarah Westwood – the result of the long investigation has been to satisfy a very attentive jury that you have been guilty of the crime of murder – of murder perpetrated by the foulest means and against him whom it was your duty to protect instead of to attack. I can hardly conceive a case of greater aggravation or enormity. In cases of murder perpetrated by violence there are at hand comparatively easy means of detection, but it is only by the advance of science and greater knowledge of scientific subjects that guilt like yours can be investigated, and when investigated and discovered it is pre-eminently the case in which the law is bound to interfere with the severest vengeance. I speak not these words in order to reproach or upbraid you, but in order that, by pointing out to you the extent and enormity of your guilt, I may influence you as far as I can to employ a few hours of life which yet remain to you in endeavouring to do all you can in this world to prepare for another. The sentence of the court upon you is that you be taken from hence to the place from which you came, from thence to the place of execution, and that you be there hanged by the neck till you be dead, and that your body, when dead, be buried within the precincts of the prison, according to the form of the statute in such case made and provided.

On hearing her sentence, Sarah Westwood fainted, then on coming round, began to moan and groan, protesting her innocence again. As a final attempt to wriggle out of her sentence, she claimed that she was pregnant, as a pregnant woman could not be hanged.

The courtroom officials immediately locked the courtroom doors to prevent people from leaving, so that they could pick a jury of twelve married women (or 'matrons'), who were then asked, along with a surgeon, to examine Sarah to see if her claim was true. It was not. She was taken to Stafford Gaol to await execution.

While there, she is supposed to have been visited by Phillips, pretending to be her brother-in-law. She claimed innocence until the very end, repenting all her sins to the prison chaplain, but stating that she could not repent of the sin of having killed her husband because she had not done it.

The Times of the 16 January 1844, using the headline 'execution of a murderess' described Sarah Westwood's last few minutes:

She appeared deeply distressed as she approached the scaffold, and when placed under the fatal beam trembled violently. The preliminaries having been quickly arranged and the rope placed round her neck, the bolt was drawn, and the sufferings of the murderess ceased in this world. After the body had hung the usual time, it was cut down, and subsequently interred within the bounds of the prison.

CHAPTER 9

The Brough Brothers of Biddulph
1845

When I took up the hammer I had no thought of striking him with it . . .

When John Brough killed his brother Thomas, there is little doubt it was the more unpleasant of the two men who had died.

Thomas Brough was not held in the highest of esteem by either his family or locals. According to the *Staffordshire Advertiser* of 5 April 1845:

> *It appears from the statements of the sister [Judith Brough] which are corroborated by persons resident in the neighbourhood of Biddulph that the deceased Thomas Brough was a selfish and unprincipled man, conducting himself with great cruelty towards his mother and other relatives. He defrauded them, it is said, of property, which should have descended to them from his father and his grandfather on the mother's side.*

The same edition of the newspaper is, on the other hand, much more generous about the murderer than the victim:

> *John Brough . . . is represented to have been kind to his mother, and of a quiet and mild disposition. Mr Passman felt so strongly the conviction that it was under a sudden impulse, provoked by his brother's unnatural conduct, that John Brough committed the fatal deed, that he forwarded, on Tuesday last an application to Mr Baron Platt for a respite, for the unfortunate man, in order that the case might undergo further consideration, and if possible, that the punishment might be commuted to transportation for life.*

The Brough brothers lived on adjoining farms. Thomas, the older of the two, farmed at High Bent Farm, while John worked Whitefields. Thomas owned both farms and John, who also looked after their widowed mother, rented his farm from his older brother. For whatever reason, John began to build up debts with his brother Thomas – the most likely explanation being that he had fallen into arrears with his rent. By the end of 1844, John owed around £30 and Thomas, who by all accounts was ill-tempered, had lost any semblance of patience. Tired of trying to procure what he was owed, on the afternoon of Friday the 3 January 1845, Thomas sent the bailiffs in on his own brother.

As there was still no money forthcoming, the bailiffs boxed up various items that belonged to both John and their mother and took them off to Thomas's house at High Bent Farm. John was furious at his older brother, arguing that he had no right to take these things. When Thomas left in the early evening to return home, John left with him. It was about 6 o'clock in the evening. Within 10 minutes, Thomas was dead. John Brough's confession makes it quite clear what happened:

> *From the time that Thomas and me went out of the house at the Whitefield farm to the time I was in again, I am certain that 10 minutes had not elapsed. It was only 2 minutes' walk to the spot where Thomas laid after I had struck him. I did not go out of my way to get the hammer I hit him with, but I went close to it as Thomas and me walked to the meadow. When I took up the hammer I had no thought of striking him with it, I am sure. It was in consequence of Thomas's saying at last (after I had begged him again and again to let me have the boxes that night) 'It is of no use your speaking any more about them, you shall not have them again tonight' – it was this that aggravated and provoked me, and caused me to hit him. Thomas was very angry when I kept asking him for the boxes. If it was the last word I had to speak, I declare that I had no intention to strike him until the moment when I gave him the blow. Why I took up the hammer, I am not able to say . . . I wanted to go with Thomas and fetch the boxes from his house that night, because I did not like to be seen by folks carrying them in the daytime. I did not wish any other person to know about my brother*

taking them off. I declare . . . that if Thomas had allowed me to have them that night, I should not have hurt him. I had never intended to strike him.

Thomas's wife, Hannah, was meanwhile preparing dinner at High Bent Farm and had been expecting Thomas home for some while. When he failed to return by 6 o'clock, her nephew had a quick look for him but with no success. When, at 9 pm, Thomas was still missing, she guessed there was a real problem. She continued searching for him herself until 3 o'clock the following morning. Meanwhile, down at Whitefields, John Brough was unable to sleep and spent most of the night sitting up by the fire.

Thomas Brough's body was found on the Saturday at Gledelow Sand Pit. He had suffered several massive blows to the head. Soon afterwards, a hammer was found in a field at Whitefield Farm. The hammer was covered in blood and had hairs matted to its surface. It belonged to John Brough. When shown the hammer, John immediately confessed to his brother James what he had done. In fact, the Police initially arrested both John and James, although James was soon released.

There was never any doubt that John Brough had committed the crime. However, it would seem to have been entirely out-of-character. In fact, it may have been an act of manslaughter, but unfortunately for John Brough, he did several things that made the killing look like murder. For a start, he tried to hide the body by removing it from the field where the attack took place, to the Gledelow Sand Pit. Then, while under arrest at the *Talbot Inn* at Biddulph, he escaped. John Brough and another prisoner were handcuffed together and they broke the cuffs apart with a stone. John then hid out in a hay barn, but was soon recaptured. Finally, and probably most significantly, he had picked up the hammer before going out into the field with his brother. Had he simply found the weapon in a moment of anger, then the jury might have brought in a verdict of manslaughter. As it was, at the trial that followed, John Brough was found guilty of murdering his brother and sentenced to hang.

There is no doubt that John Brough felt a great deal of remorse for his act and knew that he had committed a terrible deed. While in prison, awaiting execution, he dictated the following letter, addressed to his mother, Mary Brough, of New Bent, Biddulph:

County Prison, Stafford, April 5th 1845.

My dearest mother, brothers and sisters, and all my relations. I am content to leave this world. May God bless and provide for you all when I am gone. By the time you get this, I shall be in eternity. I hope the Lord has pardoned all my sins, and I that I shall be saved and meet you all in heaven. Don't neglect your souls. It will comfort you to hear that I have read my Bible and good books, and prayed to God, and felt concerned about my soul more since I have been in prison than I ever did before. I have also been more content after being with the Chaplain; I should like to have lived a few years longer to have made a home for my mother and all of you. I wish mother to have the rent of the cottage at Marsh Green deducted from the rent at the Whitfield farm and what Thomas took more than he ought to have taken. I bargained with him for the Whitfield farm, to have it for £28 per year, and he said he could collect the cottage rent and deduct it, so I should have £22 to hand to him. I wish mother to have the cottage rent as long as she lives; after her death that James and Johnny should have it, and if my mother thinks proper that any others should have a share in it. I leave it to them. I redeemed the cottage at Marsh Green about 6 or 7 years before I left service, but my brother Thomas refused to redeem it. It would have gone from us all if it had not been for me. It was never my wish to hurt Thomas. Let Johnny have my clothes box. Farewell my dearest mother, brothers and sisters, and Johnny, and all my relatives, until we meet in a better world, which is the prayer of

Your unfortunate but affectionate

X (his mark)
JOHN BROUGH

All John's relatives, including Hannah, the wife of the brother he had killed, came to see him in gaol as he awaited execution, and public sympathy for him was great. Efforts were made to have his sentence reviewed – there was no automatic right of appeal then – but to no avail. A description of the execution was carried by the *Staffordshire Advertiser* of 12 April 1845:

> *The unhappy culprit passed a disturbed and sleepless night. He was visited, at a very early hour this morning, by the Rev. Chaplain, with whom he continued engaged in devotional exercises until the time when the Under Sheriff arrived, and he was delivered up into the hands of the executioner. In the course of conversation with the Chaplain this morning, he repeated what he had before said, 'that it was never his wish to hurt Thomas – he had no thought of hitting him just as he did.' He said he did not intend to murder his brother. The other parts of the sermon he liked very much He declared that he was 'content to die' and he looked to the Lord Jesus Christ for salvation. He also said that he believed his sins were pardoned. After he had been pinioned, he walked with tolerable firmness, accompanied by the officers, to the gaol lodge, but on reaching the steps leading to the drop he trembled exceedingly, and required the assistance of two of the officers to ascend. He held down his head and wept bitterly, holding his pocket handkerchief to his face. [Author's note: I'm not sure how he could hold a handkerchief to his face when his arms were pinioned. It must be a case of journalistic licence.] The last words he was heard to utter were 'I hope the Lord will have mercy on my poor soul.' The rope having being placed round his neck, the chaplain proceeded to read the customary sentences of the burial service, and when he came to the words, 'In the midst of life we are in death,' the Executioner drew the fatal bolt and the wretched culprit was launched into eternity. After hanging an hour the body was cut down and immediately interred within the precinct of the prison.*

Even the crowd, who normally liked a good execution, couldn't get particularly worked up for this one. *The Times* of 8 April 1845 reported that:

> *The mob was not so great as had been the case on previous occasions; in fact, throughout the whole, a feeling of deep commiseration was felt for the culprit.*

Despite the reputations of the two brothers, John Brough's penitence and the fact that the crime was seen by many locals in a sympathetic light, the *Staffordshire Advertiser* was not going to flinch from stating what it thought of John Brough's deeds:

> *That the crime he committed was one for which he has justly suffered the penalty of death cannot be doubted. He admitted that on the night of the dreadful deed, though his brother's conduct was aggravating, yet, that the provocation consisted merely of his obstinate determination not to return the boxes which belonged to his mother and himself, and not in any extraordinary violence of language or conduct. No doubt Thomas Brough was destitute of every feeling which a son and a brother ought to cherish: and the manner in which he resisted the appeals of his widowed and aged mother was enough to excite feelings of the utmost indignation; but that this formed any reason for or justification of the diabolical crime of murder, ought not for a moment to be countenanced; or otherwise similar deeds of blood will be of continual occurrence. The weapon used was a murderous one; the blow struck supposing only one to have been inflicted, was a deadly blow; and was it no aggravation of the fearful crime that the victim was a brother, though an unworthy brother. We refrained from expressing so decided an opinion on the subject of the justice of the verdict and sentence until after his execution; though we have all along entertained the same view of the case.*

John Brough was not the only member of his family to hang. Some 19 years later, on Boxing Day 1864, his uncle Charles Brough was also hanged for murder outside Stafford Gaol. He had bludgeoned to death a 75-year-old man, George Walker, for half-a-crown and a pocket watch.

CHAPTER 10

Arson and Murder at Ash Flats
1852

Across the bottom of the bed lay the burnt and blackened trunk of his wife's body ... a blow over the right eye, where the bone was broken, showed, however, that she also had been murdered.

On October 1852, fire broke out in a house just a few miles out of Stafford at Castle Church, on the road to Wolverhampton. According to *The Times* of 26 October of that year:

About 8.00 am information was sent to Stafford that a cottage at Moss Pit was on fire, and engines were immediately despatched to the spot. On breaking open the door of the house, the fire was discovered to have originated in one of the bedrooms, but the smoke and flame prevented any one from ascending the staircase. Ladders were then procured and holes made in the roof of the building, and the fire engines having subsequently arrived, the flames were extinguished.

The house belonged to a couple called Blackburn (although *The Times* had their names as Blackband). John and Jane Blackburn were the parents of eight children, and

... in addition to the land and buildings adjoining, were also the owners of several fields of land. Naturally of a penurious turn, and imagining the safest place for his wealth to be on his own person, Blackband invariably carried about with him a large purse of gold and it is supposed to have been the knowledge of this fact

which induced some person or persons to conceive the horrid idea of murdering the old man and woman for the purpose of possessing their wealth.

Once the firemen had extinguished the worst of the blaze and the smoke had cleared slightly, they were able to get inside the house. The sight that met their eyes in the smouldering cottage was, to say the least, unpleasant:

On ascending the stairs, the old man and woman were discovered at the further end of the room on a bedstead, still burning. Upon examination it was found that the head of Blackband had been fractured by some heavy weapon, the frontal bone being completely smashed, and the back of the head opened. The body was reduced almost to a cinder, with the exception of the head and one of the legs. The bowels, blackened and scorched with the flames, were protruding; one leg was completely destroyed and almost every mark of identity or recognition obliterated. A small portion of his trousers still remained on the lower part of the leg, but all other clothing in the room was burnt, and the gold was nowhere to be found. Across the bottom of the bed lay the burnt and blackened trunk of his wife's body – the arms and legs being entirely gone. A blow over the right eye, where the bone was broken, showed, however, that she also had been murdered.

The Police soon derived their own interpretation of events on the day based on evidence left at the burnt house. They discovered that the Blackburns slept in different rooms of the house. A staircase led from the pantry to Mr Blackburn's bedroom, while his wife's room was up another staircase in a different part of the building.

The Police found a pool of blood at the foot of the pantry steps and from this and other evidence, decided that John Blackburn had been killed in the pantry and Jane murdered while descending the other staircase. They reckoned that the two bodies had then been carried up to John Blackburn's bedroom. The subsequent fire was an attempt by the perpetrator to cover up the fact that this was a case of murder and to lead the authorities to think that the Blackburns had died in an accidental house fire. The flames had not had the chance to cover all the traces, however, and the authorities also found a dog bludgeoned to death – presumably to stop the animal from barking or attacking – and disposed of in the well in the garden, together with the axe used in the crime. The dog, however, didn't belong to the Blackburns. They had borrowed it for protection from their youngest son, Henry. The Police also discovered that the doors were locked and the key missing, so they decided it was likely that the murderer had got into the house through a window. For the Police, there was little in the way of clues:

> *The murder must have been perpetrated after daylight. At 7.30 a gentleman passed the house, when there was no sign of fire, but he observed a man walking through the adjoining field, as if from the house. It is supposed that the murderer could not have completed the deed without having marks of blood upon some part of his body or clothes, which may lead to his apprehension.*

Such was the seriousness of the crime that the Chief Constable offered a reward for information leading to the arrest of anyone involved, of between £5 and £100 (presumably the more you knew, the more you got paid). In addition, the government also offered a further £50 for information – a substantial fee in 1850s Britain.

The crime was discovered on the morning of 25 October 1852. By the evening of the same day, Henry Blackburn, the youngest son, had already been taken into custody and Charles Moore, who worked on an occasional basis for the Blackburns, doing jobs around the farm, was to appear as a witness against him. Then, on 28 October, the Police received the first of three anonymous letters, described by *The Times* as 'somewhat contradictory'. Essentially, however, they strove to implicate another of the Blackburns' sons, Thomas, in the crime. Two further letters were received on 3 and 8 November. When Police read them, they realised that whoever had written them knew more about the way in which the crime had been committed than had been made aware to the public.

On 12 November, Moore was summoned to the Police Station to make a witness statement against Henry Blackburn.

At the Station, the Police found his evidence was somewhat confusing, so Moore offered to write it down for them. They gave him ink and paper and sent him home, where he wrote down his statement. When the Police received it, they could see instantly that Moore's handwriting was identical with that of the writer of the three anonymous letters. When they subsequently searched Moore's house, they also found evidence that linked Moore to the crime scene and the letters:

> *Mr Richards, superintendent of the Borough Police, Stafford, proved the receipt by him of an anonymous letter, and stated that in searching Moore's house he found a child's toy with which the impression had been made on the wax that secured the letter, and also a box of Lucifer matches resembling in appearance those found at the Ash Flats. On examining the kitchen of the house where the murder was perpetrated, he observed on the fastening some particles of woollen stuff, of a red colour, and, on comparing it with the waistcoat worn by Moore, it was found to correspond.*

Further arrests followed. Charles Moore lived with a woman called Catherine Walsh. Her father, Edward Walsh, was implicated by Moore and when Police saw that Walsh's hands had recently been burned, they took him into custody as well. They also arrested a man called Peter Kirwan, again on Moore's testimony. By the time the case came to trial on 18 March 1853, four men stood charged with the Blackburns' murder – Peter Kirwan, Henry Blackburn, Charles Moore and Edward Walsh. There was no evidence offered against Peter Kirwan, so the Judge instructed the jury to find him 'not guilty'.

Charles Moore had accused Henry Blackburn of paying him and others to do the deed. The jury weighed up the evidence, but after an hour's deliberation, Blackburn was also found 'not guilty'. Walsh and Moore, however, were not so lucky. The jury recommended mercy for Walsh, whom they felt had played a secondary role in the events. The Judge didn't agree with the jury and sentenced both men to hang. Both men protested their innocence. There were cries for 'mercy' from the dock and Moore is reported to have been in tears.

It was only a couple of days before he was due to hang that Moore came clean. In his confession, he stated that on the

Sunday he had been to Ash Flats to milk the cow at the Blackburns' and had returned home at around 5 o'clock. Later that evening, between 11.00 and 12 o'clock, he went back to the house at Ash Flats, which was all shut up, and he got into the house through a window by the door. His confession continues:

All that was done in it was done by myself. There was no one else in it. All that I said about Henry Blackburn giving the money was not true. We had a conversation about people murdering for hire in Ireland; but it had no reference whatever to the present case. No one had anything to do with it but myself. Neither of the Blackburns nor McCormick nor Ward nor Dillon nor Kirwan nor Walsh had any hand in it. I never mentioned it to anyone but Walsh on the Saturday night. I ask forgiveness from all the people for the untruths which I have said about them. I said what I did to throw the blame off my own shoulders . . . I acknowledge the justice of my sentence, and I ask pardon of the Almighty God for the great offence I have committed and also of all those persons whom I have implicated in the matter.

Given that he could have taken others to the gallows with him, it was one of the few decent acts of his life. As a result of Moore's confession, Walsh was reprieved and, according to the *Staffordshire Advertiser*, 'was greatly excited on learning that his life would be prolonged'. Moore was executed on 9 April 1853 outside Stafford Gaol. It was a good hanging. The *Staffordshire Advertiser* reported that 'All the ground from which a view of the drop could be obtained and the windows of the neighbouring houses were studded with spectators. A number of persons also availed themselves, at a small charge per head, of scaffolding erected for the purpose in the neighbourhood of the gaol.'

CHAPTER 11

Palmer the Poisoner
1856

Whether it is the first and only offence of this sort which you have committed, it is certainly known only to God and to your own conscience.

Stafford, 14 June 1856 – a crowd of 35,000 throngs the roads around the gaol. All the best seats have been sold. Wealthier spectators have bought viewing spaces on nearby scaffolding and rooftops. Poorer onlookers clog the roads around the gaol, hoping for a glimpse of the prisoner. This particular hanging is a popular attraction, and the railway companies have laid on special trains to bring in one of the biggest crowds Stafford has ever seen. The 35,000 have gathered to witness the execution of William Palmer, who has been convicted for the murder of John Parsons Cook. It's a case that has caught the public's imagination.

Over the years there have always been cases that, for some reason, capture both press and public attention. This is one such case. It has all the ingredients: a middle-class doctor, money, gambling, sex, adultery, scandal. What more could you want? Doctors involved in murder often create a disproportionate level of interest. After all, they are supposed to save lives, not end them.

Palmer has earned the hatred of vast swathes of the British public. Yet, from a twenty-first century perspective, the evidence in the John Parsons Cook case is flimsy. Nowadays, the case would probably have been thrown out before it even came to court. One could even go so far as to describe it as a miscarriage of justice. Indeed, the poet Robert Graves, author of

I, Claudius and *Goodbye to All That,* was moved enough to write a novelised account of the case, entitled, *They Hanged My Saintly Billy* – reputed to be Palmer's mother's verdict on the death of her son.

Only a mother could describe William Palmer in those terms. The poisoning (or otherwise) of John Parsons Cook was the last in a long line of incidents surrounding William Palmer, indicating that if he hadn't hanged for killing John Parsons Cook, sooner or later he would have hanged for something else. Palmer may even have been innocent of the crime, but his gambling, womanising and philandering were far from saintly; that he was in all likelihood a serial killer, possibly responsible for as many as fifteen murders, certainly puts him more firmly in the sinner bracket.

Palmer was born into comfortable middle-class surroundings in 1824. His father was a self-made man, a timber merchant who had built up a profitable business in Rugeley. William was the seventh of eight children. They were quite a mixture. The eldest, Mary, drank herself to death. Walter was also a sot and a bankrupt. But twins George and Sarah were highly respectable, as were youngest son, Thomas – who became a clergyman – and Joseph, the eldest son, who followed his father into the timber business. Another child, also called Sarah, had died in infancy in 1822.

By all accounts, William was the apple of his mother's eye. She indulged him, and the boy was allowed to do more or less as he pleased. When William was aged 12 his father died, and from then on, any control his mother might have exercised began to evaporate. At 17, William left Rugeley Grammar School, where he had been an indifferent scholar. His mother arranged an apprenticeship with a wholesale chemist's in Liverpool. But money soon started going missing. Suspicion fell on William, who was eventually caught red-handed opening customers' envelopes and pocketing the cash. Mother, naturally enough, intervened: only by repaying the money and having younger brother Thomas take over his apprenticeship, did William avoid scandal and gaol.

In fact, William had no need to steal. On his father's death, he had inherited £7,000 – a small fortune in the early Victorian

The childhood home of William Palmer, the Rugeley Poisoner. The author

Rugeley Grammar School. An artist's impression of Rugeley Grammar School after a drawing by John Buckler (around 1824). Both William Palmer and George Edalji attended Rugeley Grammar School. The author

era, equivalent to around £450,000 in today's money. But the lure of women and gambling proved too much for William. While in Liverpool, he had begun a dalliance with a certain Jane Widnall, his landlady's daughter, and was helping to fill the coffers of bookmakers at Chester and Liverpool races.

His next career move was to become apprenticed to a Dr Edward Tylecote at Great Haywood, a village some 5 miles from his native Rugeley. Jane had also moved with her mother, who had remarried. They, too, lived at Great Haywood. In order to continue his dalliance with Miss Widnall, William developed a clever system, whereby he bribed a local youth to call him out of church to attend to 'medical emergencies'. Thus, while Jane's mother and stepfather were busy with their weekly devotions, she would be busy with Palmer.

This apprenticeship was also doomed, when William ran off with Jane, leaving a trail of debts the rest of his family had to sort out. Despite his mother's best efforts, Dr Tylecote had had enough of his wayward young apprentice and wouldn't take him back, so Mother Palmer had to secure William yet another position – this time as a student at Stafford Infirmary, from where he went to St Bartholomew's Hospital in London as a full-blown medical student. Even then, the authorities wrote to his mother, telling her that his son stood little chance of passing his medical examinations, as he was spending most of his time drinking, singing and womanising. She paid for a crammer, Dr Stegall, to coach him – at the enormous cost of £100 (over £6,000 by today's reckoning) – and somehow William passed his final medical exams. Poor Dr Stegall. In keeping to the Palmer tradition, the family failed to pay him and he was forced to sue them for the money.

The newly qualified Dr William Palmer set up a surgery in Market Street, Rugeley in 1847. While the practice seems to have done reasonably well, Palmer's name was starting to become linked to various scandals. Rumours were circulating that Palmer was involved in an affair with a Mrs Abley. This might not have meant so much had Mr Abley not died on a drinking session with Palmer and another friend the previous year. The Coroner reported that Abley died of natural causes, but tongues were wagging.

It is hard to say with certainty that Abley was the first of Palmer's victims. Indeed, it's hard to pin down who, in Palmer's circle, died of natural causes and who died at Palmer's hands. What is certain, is that a good number of Palmer's friends, family and acquaintances were to die suddenly over the next 9 years, before George Smith, the Dudley Hangman, put a noose around Palmer's neck.

In the same year as he opened his surgery, Palmer also married Annie Brookes. Annie was the daughter of a retired

Grave of George Abley, St Michael and All Angels' Church, Colwich. William Palmer had an affair with Mrs Abley. In retrospect, Abley may well have been one of Palmer's victims. Abley shares the grave with his grandson.

The Lamb and Flag, *Little Haywood. George Abley died here after a drinking session with William Palmer. The coroner reported 'exhaustion, the result of diseased blood vessels of the lung', but ...* The author

army colonel (who owned property in Stafford) and his house-keeper, Mary Thornton. Annie and her mother had income from the various properties, which included the *Noah's Ark* public house. Mary Thornton didn't survive long into her daughter's marriage. On Twelfth Night 1849, she was found wandering the streets in a state of delirium. She was taken home and put to bed, where she died a couple of days later.

Rumours were already growing about Palmer. A story was doing the rounds that Mary had once accused him of trying to poison her. She had been ill on one occasion and Palmer had given her tablets as a 'cure'. Recovering without the need for the tablets, Mary had thrown them out of the window, where they had been eaten by her chickens – all of which died. She'd also accused Palmer of poisoning her cats. It was pure hearsay – Mary was a heavy drinker, and these stories may have been flights of fancy – but by the same token, Palmer might reasonably have expected Annie to inherit Colonel Brookes's Stafford properties, which would have been a strong motive for getting

The Surgery, *Stafford. When the* Noah's Ark *it was owned by Palmer's mother-in-law. He hoped his wife would inherit it upon her death, but that was not to be!* The author

rid of her. In the end, the Palmers didn't benefit from Mrs Thornton's death to the extent they might have hoped. After a tussle, the courts awarded Annie the income, but the properties went to a Mr Shallcross.

Whether he poisoned Mary Thornton or not, Palmer would certainly have been disappointed not to have inherited those properties. By now, his medical career was largely on hold, as he spent more time running his own stable of horses or at the racetrack. It was here he came across the next of his acquaintances to meet a sudden and painful end. One of Palmer's horse racing pals was Leonard Bladen. Palmer already owed Bladen money. After a good day at Chester races, Bladen wrote to his wife, telling her that with the money Palmer owed him, and his good fortune at the track, he should soon be bringing back around £1,000 (worth about £60,000 today): but first, he would stop off in Rugeley with Palmer for a few days, before making his way home.

Bladen never made it home. He fell ill at Palmer's house and took several agonising days to die, during which time his wife was sent for. Palmer himself signed the death certificate. Of the £1,000, there was no sign. Nor was there any sign of the betting books, in which Bladen kept the records of all his gambling. Palmer maintained he had paid his debt to Bladen, who had managed to fritter away the money in the few short days he'd been in Rugeley.

At first, Mrs Bladen was not suspicious. Indeed, she was grateful for the apparent care Palmer took in ministering to her dying husband. Later, when Palmer was awaiting trial, she would begin to have doubts, probably fuelled by salacious newspaper stories surrounding Palmer, in which rumour became fact and hearsay became the absolute truth.

Bladen's death was only the first of several that were to take place in the Palmer house over the next few years. Between January 1851 and January 1854, four of Palmer's five children died in infancy, surviving only between 7 hours and 10 days.

Inscription on the grave of Leonard Bladen in St Augustine's Churchyard. Bladen was probably another of Palmer's victims, dying in Palmer's house with a lot of money in his pocket – money that was never found. The author

The deaths were certified as due to 'convulsions', although Palmer's cleaning lady, Matilda Bradshaw, claimed that he'd poisoned them. Talk like this certainly couldn't have helped Palmer's cause. Infant mortality was far more widespread than it is today, and in 1850 the average life expectancy was just 41 years, pulled down by childhood deaths.

Meanwhile, mortality continued to stalk Palmer's friends and family. William's uncle, Joseph Bentley, died after he and Palmer had been out drinking together – a fatality following a night on the tiles seems a common theme in the mysterious and suspicious fatalities that surrounded William Palmer. Then, in September 1854, Palmer's wife Annie died as well. Like Palmer's racing pal Bladen, she died in some agony. She'd caught a chill and Palmer took it upon himself to look after her. Like Bladen, Annie had convulsions and vomiting, although her death certificate, signed by an 80-year-old doctor colleague of Palmer's, gave the cause of death as 'English cholera'.

Taken on its own, Annie's death might not have been particularly significant. However, the previous April Palmer had taken out a policy on Annie's life insuring her for £13,000 (over £800,000 in today's money). He had paid only one premium of £760. A pay-out of almost twenty times the premium would certainly help soften the blow of Annie's loss. If Palmer did grieve for his dead wife, it was only for the shortest of periods, for almost 9 months to the day that Annie died, the Palmers' maid Eliza Tharme gave birth to a child. William was the father. Curiously enough, this baby also died, aged 5 months, while under Palmer's care.

We must suppose that Palmer reasoned that if insurance companies would pay out once, then they would pay out more often. His next scam involved his brother Walter. Walter had fallen on hard times and was up to his eyeballs in debts and drink. Palmer decided his brother could not last long at the rate he was drinking, so there might be the chance of cashing in on another life assurance policy. But what doctor would certify Walter as fit? Palmer devised a plan to clean up Walter, so he could convince an insurance company his life was worth insuring. He approached six different companies and eventually managed to secure a policy worth £14,000 on Walter's life.

Palmer promised Walter £400 if he could stay sober long enough for the doctor to pass him as fit. Of the money promised, Palmer gave his brother only £60 in cash, but organised unlimited credit at a local pub. Essentially, Palmer had given his brother the wherewithal to drink himself to death. What's more, a Tom Walkenden, employed by Palmer to keep Walter sober for the insurance company, was also present at his death in the August of 1855. To rub salt into Walter's widow's wounds, Palmer visited her in Liverpool and demanded she repay all kinds of debts the poor woman had never even heard of. She stood firm and refused to pay him. Neither did the insurance company, who had already just paid out £13,000 to Palmer for the death of his wife. Instead, they sent out a couple of investigators, who were later to prove Palmer's downfall.

Not content with two insurance scams, Palmer embarked on a third. George Bates was a local farmer who, having hit financial difficulties, had given up his farm to work for Palmer, overseeing his horse stud and looking after his farming interests. Palmer, in collusion with a local solicitor and the Rugeley postmaster, Samuel Cheshire, contrived to pass Bates off as a gentleman farmer to the Midland Insurance Company. The solicitor broking the deal would make 5 per cent commission and Bates was promised £2,000 when the insurance of £10,000 was paid. Poor Bates couldn't have been the sharpest tool in the box, as he hadn't quite grasped the concept that he had to be dead in order to get his money!

Two inspectors, a Mr Field and a Mr Simpson, were sent to investigate the proposal. Palmer's little group told them that Bates was a wealthy farmer with a well-stocked wine cellar, who was free of debt and had a substantial annual income. But the two inspectors spotted Bates, dressed in near-rags, going about some mundane business. He was obviously no gentleman, so they turned down the proposal. Bates was lucky. If his life had been insured, it is unlikely he would have lived more than a few months. Less lucky was another of Palmer's friends, John Parsons Cook, who was also one of the gang trying to hoodwink Bates. Indeed, it was for Cook's death that Palmer would hang.

Cook was another of Palmer's coterie to die after a drinking session with the Doctor. The two men had been at Shrewsbury races, along with Samuel Cheshire, and were at dinner, drinking heavily. Cook swallowed a glass of brandy, which he claimed burned his throat, retiring to bed claiming that he wasn't feeling very well. The next day, the men returned to Rugeley and Cook booked into the *Talbot Arms*, near Palmer's house. Cook took to his bed again, getting up in the evening to dine with Palmer. He still wasn't well, however, and over the next few days both Palmer and the doddering Dr Bamford, who had signed Annie's death certificate, ministered to him.

Palmer seemed most concerned about his friend and sent over some broth. Cook wasn't up to eating it and the chamber-maid, not wanting to see it go to waste ate some herself. She was later to testify that she was sick after eating it. While Cook was on his sickbed, Palmer took the opportunity to slope off to London with Cook's betting books. There he recovered several of the debts noted in it. On his return, Palmer continued to visit Cook and gave him pills – supposedly morphine – to help with

Grave of John Parsons Cook in St Augustine's Churchyard, Rugeley. It was for the murder of Cook that Palmer was hanged. The author

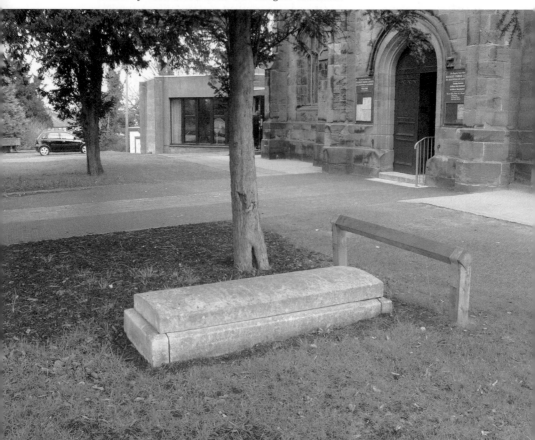

the sickness. He also called another friend, Doctor Jones, who then stayed in Cook's room to look after him. But at midnight on 21 November, Cook called for Palmer, who arrived very quickly and fully dressed, which gave rise to suspicion later. He gave Cook another two pills, declaring them to be ammonia, which aroused further suspicion: apparently, ammonia pills evaporate quickly and so were made up on demand, rather than stored ready-made.

Cook died a painful, convulsive death. No-one suspected murder at this point, as Cook had been ill for several days. But it wasn't long before the suspicions of Cook's stepfather, William Stevens, who didn't like Palmer anyway, were aroused. Stevens and Dr Jones went to Lutterworth in Leicestershire, to try to trace the will, but returned to Rugeley empty-handed to find that Palmer had already ordered Cook's coffin. Palmer also told Stevens that Cook had outstanding bills of £4,000, although no one could corroborate this fact. Stevens was now wary and couldn't find Cook's betting book, which doubled his suspicions. He asked the coroner for an inquest and a Dr Harland from Stafford was commissioned to do the post-mortem. Stevens then returned to London to consult a solicitor about Cook's financial affairs.

A modern post-mortem is carried out on strict medical and legal guidelines. But Cook's first post-mortem was more like a circus act. A small crowd was allowed to watch as Charles Devonshire, a medical student, and Charles Newton, a chemist's assistant, performed it in a public room of the *Talbot Arms*. The body was hacked about and samples removed from the room and then returned, with no knowledge of what had happened to them while out of sight. Indeed, it was such a farce, even by the standards of the times, that a second one was carried out a few days later at the request of a Dr Taylor, from St Guy's Hospital in London, who had been asked by Stevens to analyse samples.

Palmer then discovered that Dr Taylor was writing to the coroner. He got his postmaster friend, Samuel Cheshire, to intercept letters from Dr Taylor. Palmer also appears to have tried to bribe the coroner with various gifts, urging him to record a verdict of death by natural causes.

The Shrew, *Rugeley. Formerly known as the* Talbot Arms, *it figures twice in this book. It was here that the body of Christina Collins was brought after being found in the canal. Room 10 was where John Parsons Cook died of poisoning at the hands of William Palmer.* The author

Following the two post mortems, there was an inquest in mid-December in Rugeley Town Hall. Dr Taylor basically declared that although there was no trace of poison, Palmer had administered strychnine in the pills he'd given Cook during his illness. How he could square this circle is difficult to understand, but as a result the coroner's jury took only a few minutes to declare that Cook had been poisoned and that William Palmer had done it, although their responsibility was simply to decide on the cause of death, not who might be responsible for it.

Palmer was now on the slippery slope to the gallows. Following the outcome of the inquest, he was finally arrested at his Rugeley home on Saturday, 15 December 1855. They didn't have to look far to find him. Palmer was in bed ill, and already under house arrest for forgery, on a warrant taken out on him by a money-lender. The next day, he was moved to Stafford Gaol and, because of the local interest aroused in his case, he was the first prisoner to be deliberately moved elsewhere in the country to be tried.

Although he might well have been investigated for other crimes, Palmer was only tried for the murder of John Parsons Cook. In fact, on the recommendations of the two insurance investigators, Field and Simpson, the bodies of Annie and Walter were exhumed. While Walter's body had quickly deteriorated in the lead-lined coffin Palmer had paid for, Annie's body was still in good condition and when the stomach and intestines were tested for poison, traces of antimony were found. A coroner's jury found that she had been murdered. However, as Palmer was already standing trial for the killing of John Parsons Cook, no further charges were brought against him.

The trial started on 14 May 1856 at the Old Bailey. Palmer didn't stand a chance. In those days, there was no such concept as 'contempt of court', so newspapermen freely interviewed witnesses and there were daily articles about the 'Rugeley Tragedies', in which fact, opinion and hearsay were mingled to slant public opinion against Palmer. As for the evidence, it was highly confusing. Both the defence and the prosecution called expert witnesses who disagreed on the cause of death: the defence stated that if Cook had died of strychnine poisoning, there should be traces of strychnine in the body; the prosecution's case was that Cook had been poisoned, but no traces could be found because of the unprofessional post-mortem. Meanwhile, a doctor's assistant and a chemist's assistant both declared they had sold Palmer poison before Cook's death, but neither had kept a record as was the custom. And as for the chambermaid who reported being ill after consuming the broth sent to Cook by Palmer, it was fairly obvious she had been coached in her statement to the court. Finally, witnesses who might have been able to provide Palmer with an alibi were never found or simply not called.

If the cards were already stacked against Palmer, it didn't help that the prosecution barrister was one of the finest orators of the day. Sir Alexander Cockburn knew that the Palmer trial would be his last case before he became a judge. He saw it as a chance to leave on a high note. His summing-up took 6 hours, during which he used no notes. If Palmer might have got away with it before Cockburn's speech, he certainly wasn't going to afterwards. The trial lasted 12 days, with conflicting medical evidence, but the jury needed only slightly more than an hour to reach their verdict. Of course, there was no Court of Appeal. Palmer would hang.

In reality he was unlucky to hang for that particular crime – the case would have never come before a modern court – but you can take your pick from the many others it looks highly likely that he committed. Certainly the trial Judge was scathing about Palmer's behaviour. In his summing up, with his black cap on his head to denote pronouncement of the death sentence, Lord Chief Justice Campbell described Palmer's crime in these terms:

> *The case is attenuated with such circumstances of aggravation that I do not dare touch upon them. Whether it is the first and only offence of this sort which you have committed, it is certainly known only to God and to your own conscience. It is seldom that such a familiarity with the means of death should be shown without long experience; but for this offence of which you have been found guilty your life is forfeited.*

Justice Campbell sent Palmer back to Newgate to be transferred to Stafford Gaol to await execution. As a final act of luxury, Palmer travelled in a first-class compartment from Euston to Stafford.

Stafford Gaol, Palmer's home until he hanged, was no Garden of Eden, as can be seen from *The Times* report of the trial of William Palmer, which describes conditions at the county gaol and House of Correction of Stafford:

> *The grass seems to know it is in prison, or else the ground is on criminal allowance, and allowed no luxuries, such as manure; for the governor's garden is not flourishing, and beyond some remarkably fine flint stones, seems to grow nothing worthy of notice. A pathway from hence leads to the debtors' airing courts, a large piece of ground, surrounded by wooden railings. The bake-house is next to the debtors' court; and through the windows, may usually be seen*

a vast amount of bread, not in square loaves as freemen eat, but slabs of bread, like 3-inch deal planks, sawn in lengths of 3 feet, and piled together with the greatest order. A kind of grinding noise is heard, together with the hum of machinery. The power by which the millstones are put in motion, is no other than a tread-wheel of 32 felon power, with poor wretches dressed in their prison grey, walking up 'the endless stairs', which turns beneath their feet.

No doubt this would have been hard on the pampered, narcissistic Palmer, who was used to having whatever material comforts he fancied, no matter who was footing the bill. However, he didn't have to stay there too long. On 14 June 1856 he was taken outside the prison gate and there, before that baying horde of 35,000, he was hanged. Among the vast crowd, hawkers, peddlers and traders would have been out in full force selling their wares, including 'broadside ballads'. These were hastily written lines of doggerel that pretended to be morality tales, but were essentially designed to titillate. The broadside ballads for Palmer included such lines as:

Oh listen unto William Palmer
Who does in anguish sore bewail
Now guilty they at last have found me
And sent me back to Stafford Jail.
Every one appears against me.
Every person does me hate,
What excitement is impending
On guilty William Palmer's fate.

Palmer had no doubt enjoyed an enviable lifestyle of wealth, comfortable taverns and a succession of willing women. The British public loves a good fall from grace. In the trial and execution of William Palmer, they had everything they wanted – a good middle-class murder, involving lashings of sex, intrigue, financial wheeler-dealing, gambling and, to finish it off nicely, some retributive justice. Even today, 150 years after his death, the Palmer legend lives on. Since his execution, he has featured in books, postcards, poems and a TV film. He and his Rugeley house have even been recreated as Staffordshire pottery ornaments.

No doubt a great deal of interest in the case was generated by press reports. Britain was slowly becoming a literate country, thanks mainly to Sunday Schools, as compulsory education was still a generation off. The Palmer inquiry was coloured by the way it was reported in the press, and to an extent, it was a case of trial by media. The public lapped it up, and it still makes for a juicy story today.

CHAPTER 12

The Baby in the Newspaper
1865

*It will be recollected that
Mr G F Griffin, the reputed father
of the child, was alleged to have
thrown the body out of the railway
train into the river ...*

On Saturday, 23 September 1865, a group of children made a macabre discovery in the Mawddach Estuary near Dolgellau. They were playing on the river bank when they came across a bundle wrapped in paper, inside part of a pillowcase tied with string. When they removed the layers, they found the body of a baby. They ran to their parents to report the grim find: soon after, the Police arrived and took away the body for the coroner to make his report. Meanwhile, according to *The Times* of 4 October 1865:

> *In the interim most important evidence was obtained, a clue being obtained from the name on the local newspaper in which the body of the deceased infant was wrapped – the name being 'Mr G F Griffin' ... and upon Captain Clough making enquiries he found that Mr G F Griffin was well known at the* Ship *Hotel, where he had stayed on several occasions. He was also well-known at the post office where he had called for letters on his visits to Wales.*

There seemed no doubt that the dead baby was linked to George Francis Griffin. Griffin was a well-respected businessman. He had commercial interests in the area, having shares in a mining company, and was part of a family highly esteemed in his home town of Stafford. His father was, according to the newspapers of the day, 'the most respected magistrate in

Stafford Railway Station. This is the fourth station on or near the site. It was here that George Griffin bought the first-class railway ticket to Dolgellau – an occurrence rare enough to be of note to the ticket clerk. The author

Stafford', and had been Mayor of Stafford on three occasions. How could an establishment figure be connected with the body of a tiny infant discovered in such bizarre circumstances?

> *Further enquiries showed that Mr G F Griffin went to the railway station at Stafford, taking with him a portmanteau, about 12.30 on Friday week, and took a return ticket for Dolgelly, and the circumstance was especially noted as being the first through ticket issued at the station. About 2 miles from Dolgelly the railway passes close to the river Mawddach, and it is supposed that while passing the spot Mr G F Griffin threw the bundle containing the dead body of the child into the water and the tide must have carried the bundle down and across the river to the place where it was found.*
>
> *It was further ascertained that Mr Griffin arrived at the* Ship Hotel *about 7.30 on Friday evening, ostensibly with the view of*

seeing a gentleman from Manchester on some mining business, it appearing that he holds some shares in an adjacent mine, and has repeatedly visited the district.

The Dolgellau Police travelled up to Stafford and . . . the result was the apprehension of Mr G F Griffin and a domestic servant or housekeeper named Thyrza Tunstall. The woman admitted that she had given birth to a child on Thursday the 21st inst., and had thrown the placenta down the water closet. Search being made, her statement was verified, and medical examination of her person proved that she had been recently confined.

George Griffin and Thirza Tunstall (the newspaper had misspelled her name) were arrested and charged with concealing the birth of a child. Bail was set at £1,000 for Griffin (of which he stood half) and £200 for Thirza, her sureties being provided by another magistrate's son and Mr John Cooper, who was Griffin's managing agent. Meanwhile, the inquest in Wales was examining, 'The Charge against a Stafford Tradesman':

*The adjourned inquest upon the body of the female infant child which was found on the 23rd ult. on the banks of the river Mawddach, near Dolgelly, was held at Dolgelly on Wednesday. It will be recollected that Mr G F Griffin, the reputed father of the child was alleged to have thrown the body out of the railway train into the river on his way from Stafford to Dolgelly. After hearing several additional witnesses the Coroner intimated his opinion that there was not sufficient evidence to justify a verdict of wilful murder against Mr G F Griffin or any other person. The jury, after deliberating for nearly 30 minutes, returned an open verdict to the effect that the child was found dead on the bank of the Mawddach, but there was no evidence to show how it came by its death. Mr Mottram stated that, as certain reports had been circulated tending to Mr Griffin's prejudice, he should have been prepared to prove beyond all question, had the case gone any further, that at the time the child was born Mr Griffin had been absent from home 2 or 3 days, and that he never heard of the child's birth until he heard of its death. (*The Times, 6th October 1865)*

If one speculates that Griffin acted in order not to provoke scandal, then what of poor Thirza? Not only had she given

Sushions Manor farm. George Francis Griffin was arrested here while shooting with friends in 1865. The author

birth, but the baby had died and all of this in the most extraordinary circumstances. One can only guess at what the girl had been promised. Thirza was a Griffin family servant and the story of her relationship with the son of the household is one so frequently heard (there's a variation in Defoe's novel *Moll Flanders*), that it has become almost a cliché, except for the fact that there was a very human tragedy at the core of it.

The Times of 25 October 1865 reported the following, when Benjamin Thomas Oswell, the superintendent of Police at Stafford, with John Griffin his father and Police from Merionethshire, called at the Griffins' house and spoke to the girl. Oswell's testimony ran:

> *When there the prisoner cried, and appeared to be very much distressed, and said 'I beg Mr Griffin you'll forgive me.' I then began to search the room and Ann Dyche [another of Griffin's*

servants] came in. The prisoner said, 'Oh Ann, whatever shall I do?' and, 'Oh Ann, if you'd only stayed in the room that morning this would not have happened. I did not know I was so ill. I think I saw it breathe, and I fainted and fell on the floor.'

Oswell then searched the room for the missing part of the pillowcase in which the baby had been wrapped.

She [Thirza] said 'Oh I don't think you'll find it, for I cut it up and threw it down the closet in the yard . . . Don't you think it's a great shame that Mr George should be liberated? . . . Oh, Mr Oswell, you may take me into Wales and do what you like with me there; but don't let me go into this gaol, for I shall break my heart if ever I enter Stafford prison . . . don't go yet; don't leave me alone, for I feel quite alone, now that Mr George has turned his back upon me and wants to put the whole of the blame on my shoulder. But he shan't; it's his child, and he ought to have married me and not to have let his disgrace fall upon us both.'

Decently enough, Oswell warned Thirza about saying too much, as he would be acting for the prosecution and that whatever she told him could be used as evidence in the court, but Thirza pressed on, obviously fearing that she stood a good chance of being the scapegoat in the whole business:

Well, Mr Oswell, I'll tell you the whole truth about it, for I'm not going to be sent to gaol while he's at liberty, and, perhaps laughing about the matter. You must know that about a year and a half ago Mr George was ill and confined to his bed, and I had to wait upon him night and day. As he recovered he took liberties with me. Some months ago I thought something was the matter and I told him so. He said I was frightened; it was all nonsense. I told him so again, and at last he advised me to put a ring upon my finger and go to Birmingham and see a surgeon and be examined. I never did go. I could not make up my mind. I had medicine from Dr Lomax and Averill's and at last on the Wednesday I was very poorly indeed, and on that day Mr George went to his brother's. I was very ill all that night and next morning, and about 10 o'clock I had the child. I thought I saw it breathe. I fainted and fell on the floor, and when I came to myself I thought the baby was dead, and put it under the bed. I then got into bed, fearing the servants would come into the room, as they knew I was poorly. I lay in bed all that day, and when Mr George came home at night I met him in the passage and told him what had happened. He asked me if the baby was dead, and I said I thought it was, and I had hidden it under the bed. I said, 'Mr George, you must not think of going away to Wales tomorrow, and leave me in this state, for I'm afraid the other servants will find out.' He said he had an appointment and he must go, and he thought he had better take the baby with him. The next morning I put the baby in the bag, he had wrapped it in some newspapers. I took it to Mr George's dressing room and gave it to him. He wrapped it in some brown paper and then tied it up. He left for Wales by the midday train, and soon after he was gone I began to think the name might be upon the newspaper. This made me very uneasy, and I never rested until he returned on Tuesday night, when I asked him what he had done with the baby. He said, 'Oh, it's all right. I've thrown it into the sea.' I told him how I had worried myself about the name being upon the newspaper, and he said 'Pooh! Pooh! It's all right, it's only in pencil, and the water will soon wash that out.' I then rested contented and Oh! Mr Oswell, whoever would have thought this could have been found out. However, when I get out of this I'll never come back to Stafford again. Mr George ought to marry me or settle something upon me for life. Don't you think he ought?

The trial of Thirza Tunstall and George Griffin was set to take place in Merionethshire. At the Assizes in Bala, 'the court was densely crowded, and numbers were unable to gain admission,' according to the *Staffordshire Advertiser* of 24 March 1866. Thirza pleaded 'guilty' to the charge of concealing the birth of her baby. George Griffin pleaded 'not guilty'. Thirza was made to leave the courtroom while the Judge heard the whole case, although she was later called as a witness to the prosecution of Griffin. Among the others called to give evidence was Ann Dyche, another of Mr Griffin senior's servants. She told the court that:

On the 21st September she went for some medicine for Thirza Tunstall. The prisoner [George Griffin], who lived with his father, went away from home that day. Tunstall had been in the service of Mr Griffin about 5 years. She remembered Tunstall being very ill on Thursday morning, the 21st September. She fetched medicine for her and supplied her with hot salt bags and hot water for application. Tunstall was in the habit of using those remedies. She was attending to her work as usual up to the Wednesday night and although the witness was well acquainted with the figure and habits she saw nothing which led her to suspect that she was about to become a mother. The prisoner left home on Wednesday and did not return home until late Thursday night. In cross-examination the witness stated that Tunstall had suffered periodically for a disease peculiar to women.

In fact, Thirza was on the point of giving birth. Shortly after the birth, when Griffin returned home, Thirza wrote a note to Griffin asking him to come and see her, but:

He did not come to me as requested but I went to him at 2 o'clock in the night. I told him that I had had a baby in the morning and that nobody knew anything about it. I asked him what was to be done and begged him not to go into Wales and leave me in that way. He asked me if I was all right, and whether he should send for Mr Lomax, the surgeon. I asked him to let me call in the cook and get it buried at the cemetery, but he said 'No, for it will be all over the town.' He said he was obliged to go to Wales and he would take it with him.

Thirza had not realised that she would be called as a witness against Griffin and attempted to show some sort of loyalty towards him. She testified that, 'I always said I should plead guilty, but I never said before that I should be a witness. I was told that there was a sum of money offered to me to say nothing at all about it. It was one of the magistrates who offered me some money.' The matter of the alleged bribe was quickly brushed aside. Who knows if it were true or not, but there must have been some temptation among the magistrates of 1860s Stafford to look after one of their own by buying the girl off.

Griffin's solicitors also attempted to pass all blame for the crime onto Thirza. They even tried to argue that Griffin had no idea what had been in the bundle that Thirza had given him – whereas in fact he had made up the bundle himself. Mr Baron Bramwell, the Judge, in summing up explained to the jury the object of the Act of Parliament making concealment of birth under any circumstances an offence, and said he should be:

> ... *very glad if he could find something to say on both sides in every case, because for a judge to speak all on one side had an appearance of unfairness which did not in reality exist when all the facts were upon one side. But what doubt could there be in the present case? There was the young woman's statement which they were hardly invited to disbelieve, and it was corroborated in every possible way. Moreover the prisoner when arrested did not deny the charge.*

It did not take the jury long to find both defendants guilty. Mr Baron Bramwell first addressed George Griffin:

> *I shall pass a lenient sentence and I wish to explain my reasons for it ... it was a violation of decency so to dispose of the body of what after all was one of your fellow creatures. But the child was certainly dead before you knew of its existence, and it was probably a merciful thing to the woman who was the mother of it to endeavour to suppress the fact of its birth. But the law has made it an offence to do what you have done, with the view of protecting infant life. The sentences that have been passed upon persons convicted of concealment of birth have been varied according as it was supposed the harm was done to the child or otherwise. In cases where there has been no suspicion of anything of the kind the punishment has been very slight. In your case there is no reason to suppose you did anything improper to the child, because it is manifest you did not expect it to be born at the time it was and the mother, who is the principal witness, says she had made preparations for it. While you first knew of its birth it was certainly dead ... It is impossible not to pass some sentence upon you, because being a man of education, and not having been at the time in that state of alarm and fear which women are who have had children born to them in this way, you certainly ought to have known better than to do what you did. Besides, you have broken the law, and therefore you must have a sentence passed upon you. But considering your state of health and considering all the circumstances, I sentence you to only a fortnight's imprisonment.*

If Griffin was to get away so lightly, was this because blame was going to fall more heavily on Thirza Tunstall?

His Lordship said the sentence upon her would be a nominal one. He had no authority to punish the immorality which she and the other prisoner had committed with each other; he could only punish them for the legal offence committed. She swore that she did not expect the child so soon, that she had made some preparations for it, that she advised the other prisoner to have it taken to the cemetery to be buried and that it was by his act more than by hers it was disposed of in the manner it was. He thought, therefore, not because she had been a witness for the prosecution, but because her guilt was as small as possible, the sentence upon her ought to be a nominal one. He sentenced her to a day's imprisonment which would enable her to be discharged immediately.

It was certainly an enlightened decision. But what became of Thirza after these unfortunate events? Surely scandal would have followed her for years afterwards and her prospects of a happy life must have been blighted?

During the trial, mention is made of Thirza's being engaged to a Mr Benton. Searching the records, I find that Thirza Tunstall married Francis Greensill Benton in March 1866 at St Mary's Church in Stafford. In the end, she didn't need to leave the area as she feared she would, and Francis Benton was good enough to stick by her. As far as I can ascertain, however, they had no children of their own.

As a matter of interest, her Stafford solicitor was George Palmer, brother of the notorious Rugeley Poisoner, William Palmer: at least one Palmer was on the side of decency and justice.

CHAPTER 13

William Collier: the Poacher They Hanged Twice
1866

A second time did the halter sway to and fro and again did the priest, turnkeys, culprit and hangman appear in sight of the crowd.

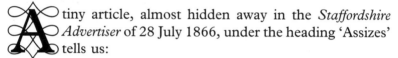 tiny article, almost hidden away in the *Staffordshire Advertiser* of 28 July 1866, under the heading 'Assizes' tells us:

> *It will be seen that the trial of William Collier, for the murder of Mr Thomas Smith jun., of Whiston Eaves near Cheadle, and which occupied the court for 13 hours on Wednesday, resulted in a verdict of guilty and the prisoner, on being sentenced to death, was emphatically informed by Mr Justice Shee not to entertain any hope that the sentence would not be carried out.*

The *Staffordshire Advertiser* was quite correct. There was no reprieve for William Collier, who was to become the last man to be hanged publicly outside Stafford Gaol. An Act of Parliament in 1868 was to ban public executions. Perhaps rumours were in the air that time was running out for this popular spectator sport, for when Collier went to the scaffold a good crowd turned out to see the show. They were in for a particularly good time as the preparations for Collier's hanging had not been as scrupulous as they might and the crowd got to see him go through the process twice. Under a headline declaring, 'Shocking Scene at Execution', *The Times* of 8 August 1866 carried a description of what happened:

> *At Stafford yesterday about 2,000 persons, chiefly from the [Staffordshire] Moorlands assembled in front of the gaol to witness*

the execution of William Collier, a young tenant farmer, who had most deliberately taken the life of Thomas Smith, jun., a young man only 25 years of age, the son of the owner of the manor at Whiston Eaves, near Cheadle.

It appears that the rope with which Collier was to be hanged was not delivered at the prison until 8.30 on Monday evening. The assistant-warders on consequence spliced a rope left after the last execution to a piece of old rope. The noose was formed of the former, and the latter was attached to the beam, round which it was twisted twice, and then the ends were fastened with string and parts of the unwound rope, but it would appear, very insecurely.

The hangman for the day was the infamous George Smith, the Dudley Higgler, who had learned his trade as assistant to the bungling William Calcraft. For years, Smith had been selling pieces of the rope that was said to have hanged William Palmer, the Rugeley Poisoner. One might have thought this hanging would have given him a good marketing opportunity for a fresh sales drive of 'the rope that hanged William Collier' and arranged for his rope to arrive in good time. However:

Smith ... pulled the drop in the usual way. The floor fell, but instead of the culprit's head being seen above the scaffold boarding it altogether disappeared. There was a cry, 'The man's down!' 'The rope's broken!' The powerful tug which resulted from the falling of the culprit through the scaffold floor had, in fact, been too much for the fastening by which the rope held to the beam. The intertwined threads became liberated, the knot slipped, and Collier fell to the ground.

It's difficult to know if Collier would have been relieved or thrown into even greater torment than he must have already felt, if indeed he could have felt anything at all, as the description continues:

For an instant there was dismay both upon and below the scaffold. The executioner was for a moment bewildered. He ran down the steps and beneath the platform and found Collier upon his feet, but leaning against the side of the hoarding, the cap over his face and the rope round his neck. He seemed to be unconscious, and the hangman turned back again, not knowing what to do.

The rule was that if a man were hanged three times and survived the drop, then he would be allowed to live. A couple of decades later, John 'Babbacombe' Lee, who was found guilty of the murder of Emma Keyse, survived three attempts to be hanged and his sentence was commuted. Perhaps for a few minutes, the semi-conscious Collier must have thought he had a chance of surviving the drop:

> *The assistant-warders, however, understood what had happened. They ran into the prison to procure the new halter that had been delivered the previous night, while others told the hangman to take the old one from Collier's neck. The hangman had now regained self-possession. He quickly took the rope off the culprit's neck, and drew the white cap from over his face. The Rev. Canon O'Sullivan, the Roman Catholic chaplain, now hurried from the platform. He was much affected. When he saw Collier fall to the bottom of the drop he buried his face in his surplice and as he afterwards hastened to continue his ministrations to the culprit, he exclaimed 'God help me!' Collier was very pale. He seemed to notice nothing whatever of what had taken place; his whole attention seemed to be absorbed in replying to the prayers repeated by the priest. The tightened rope had left a deep-red mark around his neck. While this was going on below, the assistant-warder, with the help of a ladder, again fastened the rope to the beam, and this time securely, though without any lashing. A second time did the halter sway to and fro and again did the priest, turnkeys, culprit and hangman appear in sight of the crowd. Their reappearance was the signal for an outburst of popular indignation. The hoots and calls were repeated until the drop again fell. In 2½ minutes from the time of his second fall the culprit was evidently dead. About 4½ minutes intervened between the two falls.*

Collier, a married man with seven children, confessed his guilt to the Rev. Mr O'Sullivan before the execution. The body of his victim had been found on the night of 5/6 July 1866. He was a young man called Thomas Smith, the son of a farmer of the same name, who was a large landowner at Whiston, in the parish of Kingsley, near Cheadle. The state in which the young man's body was found was described in some detail in the *Staffordshire Advertiser* of 7 July 1866:

It presented a frightful appearance, the skull having been fractured in several places and the head being covered in wounds. One of the injuries had evidently been produced by a gunshot and the others by heavy blows from some weapon, supposed to be the stock of a gun. The rigger of a gun was found under the deceased's dead body. A short distance off a ramrod was discovered and further up the wood was found the deceased's hat. This had been perforated with shot, and there were hairs adhering to it.

The Police soon had a prime suspect. William Collier was known to be at loggerheads with the Smith family and had a reputation as a poacher – hardly surprising as he had such a large family to feed. The Smiths had been plagued by poaching on their land and, on the evening in question, Thomas Smith junior had got up in the early hours of the morning with a gamekeeper as:

It appears that it was the deceased's practice to go out early in the morning to watch the preserves of his father's estate, they being occasionally frequented by poachers and it had been arranged between him and a servant that they should station themselves on Thursday morning at points about a mile apart. In accordance with this arrangement the deceased left his father's house about 3 o'clock on the morning named. He did not return and a search being made for him, his dead body was found about 10 o'clock the same morning.

Upon the body being discovered it was taken to the house of the deceased's father, and information was given to the Police. Inquiries were at once set on foot under the direction of Superintendent Woollaston, and yesterday morning the Police arrested a man named William Collier on the charge of being concerned in the murder. We understand that the Police have very cogent evidence against him.

There was, in fact, little to link Collier to the crime, even though the newspaper was ready to declare that:

Collier recently purchased of Mr Mellor of Hollington, a gun, the ramrod of which was found near the body. It has been identified by Mr Mellor as belonging to the gun which he had sold to Collier. The gun cannot be found.

Witnesses called to the trial spoke of hearing two shots in the middle of the night. One couple, Eliza and Thomas Moorcroft, seemed to have a greater part to play in Collier's conviction than most. Eliza swore that she had seen Collier moving about at 3.30 on the morning of the shooting. How she could see him and why she was awake at that time remain a mystery. However, her suspicions were aroused enough for her to send her husband out the next day and find what was deduced to be Collier's gun shoved into a culvert. This is rather a neat bit of evidence, which would not have stood up to a great deal of scrutiny.

Who owned the gun was also a matter for some debate. Collier denied that it was his, but Mellor, the gunsmith, and several other witnesses stated that the gun was Collier's, yet there was nothing to prove that this was the gun used, even if Mellor was correct in identifying both the ramrod and the gun as Collier's.

The evidence against Collier was flimsy. His confession could be seen as anything: a bit of invention on the part of the *Staffordshire Advertiser*, an attempt on Collier's part to ensure that he wasn't damned to spend eternity in the flames of hell, or possibly the truth. Whatever the true story – and one can't help but suspect the hands of Eliza and Thomas Moorcroft – Collier was not only the last man to be hanged publicly outside Stafford Gaol, he got to bear that distinction twice.

CHAPTER 14

The Deserter who Killed 1866

For the sake of a paltry gain, you cruelly murdered the man who had befriended you.

On Wednesday 14 March 1866, George Bentley, a deserter from the 17th Regiment of Foot faced the Stafford Assizes. He was charged with the murder of John Poole on 10 January of the same year. When asked how he pleaded, Bentley replied 'not guilty'.

On 11 January, the day after John Poole went missing, a young boy named Thomas Hocknell was looking for a knife he had lost somewhere in Walk Mill Road at Offley Brook. On the grass verge, he came across a man, covered in blood. A large stone, tied up inside a handkerchief lay near the body, whose only sign of life was a leg that twitched from time to time. Various items of clothing lay scattered around and the man's pockets had been turned inside out.

The injured man was moved by wheelbarrow to a nearby house and Doctor Swift from Elford Hill near Eccleshall was sent for. He later described the state in which he found John Poole:

I examined him and found four wounds on his head. The most conspicuous one was upon his forehead; it was about 1½ inch long and superficial in depth. There was a piece of plaister [plaster] upon it which I removed. It was only a slight wound. On the right temple there was a frightful contused wound, the skull having been smashed to pieces. Those fractured pieces would rest upon the brain, and the wound must have caused immediate insensibility. There was a small contused wound on the right parietal bone, and another

The lane near Offley Brook, where John Poole was found by Thomas Hocknell, barely alive. The author

on the left temple. Stimulants were employed all Tuesday, and on Wednesday morning Mr Nance and myself resorted to the operation of trepanning the deceased's skull. I considered it a hopeless case from the first, and the operation was not performed with the view of saving the deceased's life, but in the hope that sensibility might return so that he might state who was his assailant.

According to the *Staffordshire Advertiser* of 17 March 1866, which reported the trial:

The deceased John Poole was a man of about the age of 49, and was by occupation an excavator. He had emigrated to America a few years since, and hence was sometimes called 'American Jack'. Since he returned to England, he had been employed in different parts of the country, and when out of work he used to lodge at the house of his father, who lived at Croxton, near Eccleshall. On Saturday the 6th January, he went to his father, and remained there until the following Monday morning, when he left about

9 o'clock, with the intention of going to Eccleshall. He was wearing a red plush waistcoat, which would be often mentioned during the case, and in the inside pocket of this garment he had a purse containing about £1 in half-crowns and florins . . . .

It would also appear that the deceased told the prisoner in the course of conversation that he had earned £6 on a new line of railway in the neighbourhood and showed him a pair of new boots he was wearing. The deceased left the public house about 4 o'clock, and instead of proceeding in the direction of Croxton, where his father resided, he turned to the right and went down the road which led past the Walk Mill to Copmere.

That was the last time that John Poole was seen conscious. That same evening, George Bentley was already spending the money he had taken from John Poole's body. George Talbott, a draper of Eccleshall told the trial:

Between 7 and 8 o'clock on the evening on Monday 8th January, the prisoner came to my shop and bought a new slop [a kind of smock or overall] and handkerchief. He gave me two half-crowns in payment. He put the new slop on over the one he was wearing. He had a red plush waistcoat on.

He was then seen in at least two public houses in Eccleshall. First of all, he drank ale, gin and rum at the *George Inn*. The

The George Inn, Eccleshall. One of the inns on George Bentley's pub crawl after he had killed Mr Poole. The author

The Royal Oak, *Eccleshall. George Bentley was arrested here after a disturbance in the tap room.* The author

barmaid, Ann Tildesley noticed that he had a large number of coins – he even flashed the purse at her and told her that he wasn't short of money – and that he was wearing a new pair of boots that were not laced up. By the time he found his way to the *Royal Oak Inn*, he was obviously beginning to feel the effects of drink as he became involved in a disturbance in the taproom. Drinking in the other bar was a retired Police Officer, Frederick Robinson. His evidence to the court ran:

> *On the Monday evening in question I was at the* Royal Oak Inn, *Eccleshall when a disturbance arose in the taproom. At the request of the landlady I went into the room and saw the prisoner there. I went up to him and said, 'Your name is George Bentley.' He said, 'No, it's not,' and gave some other name. I said, 'It is, and you're a deserter from the 17th Regiment of Foot. I have received a description of you.' I took him into custody. He said he would give*

me a sovereign to let him go, and drawing his hand across his throat said, 'I'd rather do this than be a soldier.' Outside the house he offered me 30 shillings to let him go, but I took him to the Police Station. He refused to be searched, and became very violent. He endeavoured to hide something behind him, which proved to be a purse, containing 19s 6d, in silver, chiefly in half-crowns and 4½d in copper. Two pocket knives were found upon him. He was wearing a clean slop and handkerchief.

When he went back the next day with one of the local Police, Constable Clutton, he soon realised that the man in custody was likely to be guilty of more than deserting from the army. Frederick Robinson continued:

I turned up his coat and found that he was wearing the red plush waistcoat, which the deceased had on when drinking at the Four Crowns. There were fresh stains of blood upon it. In answer to a question I put to him, he said he had bought the waistcoat in Yorkshire. I said, 'How come this blood upon it?' He gave two short coughs, drank a little water, and then replied, 'I got that in a row at Shrewsbury.' After looking at his boots I charged him with murdering John Poole the previous night between Offley Brook and the Walk Mill, and told him that whatever he said would be given in evidence against him. He made no answer and Police Constable Clutton said, 'You hear the charge have you anything to say?' He lifted his head and said, 'I don't know nothing about that.'

Mr Mottram, who acted as George Bentley's defence lawyer, could not contradict the evidence that had been given. His tactic was to try to make the jury think the killing might have been an act of manslaughter rather than murder, asking the jury:

. . . to believe that the two men had fallen out, and had a desperate combat. The deceased, it was proved, was slightly intoxicated, and when in this state was inclined to be quarrelsome. What was more likely than that a quarrel had taken place between him and the prisoner? There was no evidence to prove that the prisoner entertained ill will towards him – on the contrary, it seemed that he had treated him with kindness, and plaistered [plastered] his head when

Offley Brook. George Bentley followed John Poole alongside the mere before killing him. The author

it was cut in the room of the public house. If a quarrel ensued something must have occurred to exasperate the prisoner and induce him to inflict such fearful injuries on the deceased. He trusted the jury would take this view of the case and find the prisoner guilty of manslaughter.

He impressed upon the jury the fact that if they did find Bentley guilty, it was a very serious charge and that he would forfeit his life. Besides, if Bentley was guilty of murder, why on earth would he remain in the neighbourhood, drinking in local public houses, rather than fleeing elsewhere in the country?

Once the Judge had summed up, it took the jury only 5 minutes to bring in a verdict. They didn't even need to leave the jury box before deciding that Bentley was guilty of murder. They must have reasoned that a killer who commits man- slaughter as part of a drunken argument, does not then strip his corpse of anything valuable, but is more likely to run away from his misdeeds. Then

> *His Lordship assumed the black cap, and proceeded to pass sentence of death. He said, 'George Bentley, the jury have found you guilty of a foul and dreadful murder. For the sake of a paltry gain, you cruelly murdered the man who had befriended you. I have only to pass upon you the last dread sentence of the law: and I implore you to use the time remaining to you in making your peace with God, whom you have so grievously offended.'*

George Bentley's crime – incompetent, vicious and stupid – aroused just enough interest to make a small piece in the national press. *The Times* of 28 March 1866 carried an article entitled 'Execution at Stafford':

> *Yesterday George Bentley, aged 27, who was condemned at the last Staffordshire Assizes for the murder of John Poole, aged 49, an excavator, was executed in front of the gaol at Stafford. A crowd assembled, consisting chiefly of young persons, numbering nearly 2,000. A body of Police 100 strong was present, under the command of Colonel Hogg, the chief constable, and Major McKnight, the deputy chief constable of the county. The culprit walked pinioned from his cell to the gallows, audibly saying a prayer taught him by the Rev. W P Vincent, the chaplain. The executioner was a man named Smith, a cattle dealer of Dudley. The culprit was seen only to move his hands twice spasmodically immediately after being turned off, and he was dead. He made a full confession in a letter addressed to the chaplain.*

Bentley's only distinction was that he got to share the same hangman as several more notorious murderers, including the infamous Rugeley Poisoner, William Palmer, probably Staffordshire's most infamous villain.

CHAPTER 15

The Motiveless Murder of Mary Kidd
1874

Could there exist a man so utterly and brutally debased as to commit such a crime?

When Robert Taylor walked out to face the hangman's noose on 29 December 1874, he was comparatively lucky. There was a new hangman on the scene, a man by the name of William Marwood, a cobbler from Horncastle in Lincolnshire.

Before Marwood, those awaiting the drop in the Midlands were likely to encounter either William Calcraft or George Smith. Calcraft was a bungler, who often used a length of rope that was too long. Consequently, the victim's neck didn't break and the malefactor would have to be finished off by one of Calcraft's assistants, pulling down on the legs to achieve the desired result. Smith had been Calcraft's apprentice, becoming a hangman's assistant by accident when Calcraft's usual help-mate failed to turn up: Smith, a debtor in the gaol, saw an opportunity to wipe his slate clean and volunteered his services. Smith followed in his master's footsteps, being only marginally less cack-handed.

But Marwood had developed a more 'scientific' approach to hanging, using weight and height calculations and a length of rope between 6 and 10 feet, adjusted according to his computation. He could ensure a swift end to the prisoner. For generations before Marwood, the sight of the prisoner twitching and swinging for many minutes after an 'execution' was not uncommon.

The advent of the railway meant that Marwood was able to travel more widely than previous hangmen. Local gaols were no longer reliant on some bodger who simply 'turned off' the occasional prisoner. Marwood could, and did, travel all over England, and occasionally plied his trade in Ireland. By the end of his time, he had hanged nearly 200 people for a variety of offences. His business card was embossed with the words: 'William Marwood – Public Executioner, Horncastle, Lincolnshire'. Marwood took a pride in his work and didn't care who knew it. He was a master craftsman.

It may have been small consolation for Taylor that he was about to be hanged by an artist – after all, he was going to die anyway – but at least he knew his end would be swift. He could also take some small comfort from the fact that public executions had been outlawed only a few years previously and that, in fact, he would only be the second man to hang inside the walls of Stafford Gaol itself. As one might expect, his forthcoming execution had certainly been preying on Taylor's mind, although it didn't seem to spoil his appetite. The reporter of the first *Staffordshire Advertiser* for the new year of 1875, writes that:

> *During his confinement in the gaol Taylor conducted himself upon the whole with remarkable composure, though at night his sleep was frequently broken and disturbed. Such mental disquietude as he may have occasionally experienced did not affect his appetite prejudicially, for he was always ready for his meals, and so long as the quantity of food was ample, did not trouble himself about the kind or quality.*

In fact, the morning before he was due to meet his maker, warders were impressed that Taylor could eat all that he managed, given his impending doom. Amongst other things on the condemned man's breakfast table was over 1 lb of meat. Strangely, into the back of the spoon he used to eat this gargantuan breakfast he scratched a small picture of a figure hanging from a gallows.

The murder that Taylor had committed to find himself on the gallows was also a strange business. It seemed entirely motiveless and pointless. It was 23 November 1874 and the day was drawing to a close. Mary Kidd, the wife of a labourer from Hoar Cross (then normally written as one word – Hoarcross), was making her way home from Yoxall. With her was a young girl, Sarah Ann Hollis, who was the daughter of one of Mary's neighbour's and only 8 years old. As they reached a small wood, not far from Mary Kidd's house, they saw a man slumped on a stile: 'Are you going to sleep?' Mary asked him. 'Yes,' replied the man. 'Then wouldn't you be better at home, where it's warm?' 'I've got never a home to go to,' said the man. Mary Kidd and Sarah Hollis continued on the path home. Suddenly, the man ran after them and stood in their way. He demanded half-a-crown (around £8 in today's money). Mary Kidd said she didn't have that much money, but if he needed help, he could have what she had on her, which amounted to 2*d*. Without saying a word, and without the slightest provocation on Mary or the child's part, the man took out a clasp-knife, opened the blade and slashed Mary Kidd across the throat. As she fell, he caught her with the knife a second time.

Whether the man had also intended killing Sarah Hollis is not known. Just at that moment, something startled Taylor. He leapt over a gate into an adjoining field and disappeared. The young Sarah Hollis ran terrified all the way home to fetch help.

On the morning following the murder, Taylor, whose description was circulating in the area, was apprehended at Burton-on-Trent. His arrest was described in detail by the *Staffordshire Advertiser* of 12 December 1874, whereby Superintendent Bowen of Burton-on-Trent took

> . . . *a statement as to what had occurred from the little girl. He went in search of the man she described. Next morning, while driving into Burton, he met the prisoner in the Branstone road. The prisoner crossed the road and went into a shop, and witness followed him and took him into custody, telling him he was charged with murdering a woman at Hoarcross by cutting her throat with a knife. Witness cautioned him in the usual form. The prisoner replied: 'All right, you'll have to prove it.' On the way to the Station he said, 'Is the woman dead?' Witness replied, 'She is,' then he said, 'I suppose they'll hang me, or someone else, for it?' At the Station witness examined him and his clothing. His right wrist*

was stained with blood, and the inside of that sleeve of the coat was stained with freshly dried blood. He had two shirts on, and both wristbands were stained with blood. There were the marks of a bloody hand on the seat of his trousers. His right arm and wrist were stained with blood, and there was a clot of blood upon one of the clogs. The prisoner was afterwards put with six other men, strangers to witness, at the Meynell-Ingram Arms Inn, *when the little girl picked him out.*

At the subsequent trial, the only possible defence that could be put forward was that of insanity. Mr Underhill argued that:

The behaviour of the prisoner in this unhappy business from first to last showed that he was of unsound mind. Reviewing the circumstances under which the homicide was committed – the absence of all provocation, the impossibility of malice – he argued an unsoundness of mind. There was no motive: not even that of robbery, for not only was there no allegation of such a motive, but the fact that he

The Meynell-Ingram Arms *at Hoar Cross. This was where Robert Taylor, the killer of Mary Kidd, was identified by Sarah Ann Hollis, the young girl who witnessed the attack.* The author

ran away when he might have stopped to rifle the body of his victim negatived such a supposition. Could they say that the act was that of a sane man? Could there exist a man so utterly and brutally debased as to commit such a crime in return for the kindness the woman had shown him unless he had lost his senses? There was evidence of mania in the fact that so soon as the taste for blood, which was a sign of insanity, was satisfied, he sprang like a maniac into the neighbouring wood and nothing more was seen of him for 30 minutes. Had he been a wilful murderer would he have left untouched the only witness to his crime, the little girl?

It was a defence that failed to swing a single member of the jury, who decided that Taylor was guilty in a matter of minutes. The *Staffordshire Advertiser* for Saturday 2 January 1875 again picks up the story:

Eight o'clock was the hour fixed for the execution. The morning was tolerably clear and the biting keenness of the frosty air added not a little to the discomfort of those whom official or professional duties compelled to be in attendance on the melancholy occasion. Marwood, of Horncastle, the appointed hangman, arrived at the prison on Monday. The gallows – the same that had been in use at the gaol for a great number of years – was placed near the carriage entrance, and looking somewhat like a huge cattle truck with a platform and stout crossbeam overhead. The convict went to bed about 8 o'clock on the previous evening, but was restless for a couple of hours when he fell soundly asleep. On rising about 4 o'clock in the morning he was at once attended by the Rev. W P Vincent. Shortly after 5 o'clock he was conducted to the chapel, where he was baptised and received the Holy Communion ... Taylor breakfasted with remarkable zest about 6.30, consuming a quart of cocoa, fully a pound of beef and a proportionate quantity of bread. Immediately afterwards he was attended by the Chaplain. At 7.45 the dismal tolling of Christ Church bell gave the first definite indication to the small crowd outside the gaol that the final scene in the convict's career was approaching. The process of pinioning, which took place in the condemned cell, was submitted to quietly and without remark, and just before 8 o'clock a procession was formed and proceeded to the scaffold.

As the procession passed along, portions of the burial service were read aloud by the Chaplain. The condemned man walked firmly and quickly over the long intervening space between the cell and the gallows, his countenance showing no sign of emotion. Having shaken hands as well as the pinioning straps would allow, with the chaplain, assistant chaplain and gaol officials, he ascended the steps with alacrity to the scaffold, on which he was attended by the chief warders and the hangman, and took his stand on the trap under the crossbeam. His coolness never for a moment forsook him. His legs having been strapped, a white cap was drawn over his face. As the rope was being adjusted the convict remarked, in an under tone, 'Snap me off quick,' a request that though needless, found literal fulfilment. Marwood bade Taylor farewell by shaking one of his hands, and in a second or two the bolt was drawn, the culprit falling a depth of fully 5 feet and completely out of sight of those standing below, to whom a slight vibration of the rope was the only sign of motion visible. Subsequent examination of the body by the gaol surgeon, Mr C H Greaves, showed that the neck was dislocated and there can be no doubt that death was almost instantaneous. Immediately after the drop fell a black flag appeared on the tower over the gaol entrance, and the bell ceased tolling.

The body of the convict was subsequently interred in a grave-yard adjoining the south-east angle of the prison chapel, where the remains of a number of other executed criminals, including the notorious William Palmer, had been formerly deposited. Tuesday's execution was the second event of the kind which had been privately conducted within Stafford Gaol, the first having been that of Christopher Edwards, who was convicted in August 1872, of the murder of his wife at Willenhall.

We shall never know why Taylor killed Mary Kidd. It was a senseless crime that gained Taylor nothing – not a penny was stolen – yet cost him his life. Perhaps he was simply insane? The jury, however, did not think so.

CHAPTER 16

Slaying Cain
1874

It was tolerably obvious therefore, that unless the man committed suicide, and undressed himself, before doing so, some person or persons must first have struck him and then thrown him down the pit ...

Ventilation to the coalface had been poor for a number of weeks. The miners working Rompin Pit in Silverdale complained to James Lucas, the manager, who then sent a group of workers to investigate the problem. They began clearing a ventilation shaft that had been untouched during the previous 8 or 9 months.

About 140 yards down the shaft, the workers came across an unpleasant surprise. One worker thought it was just a pile of rags, but it soon became obvious that they had found a body. It was in an advanced state of decay, caused by the high temperatures in the ventilation shaft. Later in court, Lucas described what he had seen: 'One arm was severed from it, and the body was perfectly naked, except that the arm attached to the body had a wristband and piece of cuff upon it. The legs were broken as if by falling.' On the scaffolding above the body was a pair of trousers, in the pocket of which was £1 1s 11d (over £60 in modern reckoning).

On investigation, it was found that the body was probably that of Cain Lawton, a miner, who at the end of the previous year had been living with his sister and her husband, Sarah and Samuel Scarratt in Finney Green. Samuel was called to identify the body and was only able to do so from the clothing and shoes found with the body and from the fact that Cain Lawton had some kind of deformity of one of his feet.

Lawton was a butty miner – a miner who moved from one colliery district to another, picking up work when and where he could. They had last seen him on the evening of 19 December 1874, when they left him drinking with a friend in a pub in Silverdale and no one else had seen him since that date. Although there had been a few whispered rumours about what had happened to him, Lawton's family had not been particularly worried about him as he drifted from one job to the next.

Lawton's death could have been accident, suicide or murder. The railings protecting the ventilation shaft meant that it was unlikely that Lawton could easily have fallen accidentally into the shaft. The coroner's report also ruled out suicide and decided that Lawton must have been murdered. The reasons were paraphrased at the subsequent trial:

> *In the ventilating shaft ... were certain scaffolds. On the lowest scaffold the body was found ... It was lying perfectly straight on its side and naked. On examination it was found that on the scaffold above were some of the deceased's clothes, and after a subsequent search other articles of his clothing were found in a bundle on the same scaffold. It was tolerably obvious therefore, that unless the man committed suicide, and undressed himself, before doing so, some person or persons must first have struck him and then thrown him down the pit, and either before or after doing so must have thrown down his clothes. If it should be suggested that his being thrown down the pit was the result of an accident it was important to remember that the pit was fenced round, and that the fence was of such a nature that it was almost impossible that any man, unless he crawled deliberately through, could have tumbled through or over it. In addition to that there was a grating or plate half over the pit mouth, affording further protection against accident.*

Eventually, from rumours circulating and talk of the last time Lawton had been seen alive, the Police felt they had enough evidence to prosecute two miners William Luke, aged 22 and John Ratcliffe, 33. They appeared before Baron Pollock in the Stafford Summer Assizes of 1875. The *Staffordshire Advertiser* of 24 July carried a blow-by-blow account of the trial, under the heading: 'Alleged Murder at Silverdale'. A local solicitor, Mr Underhill opened the case for the prosecution and stated that:

> *It would be important to consider whether the man was killed by being thrown down or falling down the pit, or whether he was killed previously to being thrown down. As far as he could gather, there was a preponderance of evidence to show that he met with his death before he was thrown down.*

Cain Lawton's final night was examined in detail by the court. On 19 December, he went out at about 7.30pm to the *Black Horse* in Newcastle-under-Lyme with Samuel and Sarah Scarratt, his sister and brother-in-law. The couple left about 2 hours later, leaving him drinking with a friend of Lawton's – Joseph Grindley. When the pub closed at 11 o'clock, Grindley and Lawton set off back for home. Shortly before midnight they called at the house of a James and Sarah Lloyd in Church Street, Silverdale to light their pipes. They didn't stay long and when they left

> *... they proceeded on again, but had not gone many yards when they came upon the prisoners and a man named Philip Rowley, One of these men, said by one witness to be the prisoner Luke, and by another witness to be Ratcliffe, spoke to him, and apparently without provocation on Lawton's part went up to him and knocked him down. Lawton and Grindley were considerably affected by liquor. Grindley assisted his companion to rise, and then Ratcliffe took off his coat, squared up to the deceased, and challenged him to fight. Grindley stepped between them, and Lawton probably knowing that he was not in a position to defend himself went down the street. After he left, a quarrel ensued between Grindley and the prisoners, and Grindley was knocked down by one of them. A bottle of rum fell out of his pocket, and the prisoners and Rowley drank some of its contents. Meanwhile the deceased was seen proceeding up Church Street on the other side of the road, as though desirous not to attract attention.*

This one-sided fight was witnessed by Philip James and Ephraim Mountford. Mountford crossed the road to help and was told, 'not to concern himself with the matter'. He also

Church Street, Silverdale. Location of the last sighting of Cain Lawton before his body was found in the Rompin Pit. The author

heard Ratcliffe say that 'He would be Cain Lawton's *******
butcher':

> *The deceased was seen to pass up towards the church gates, and at a point where there is a bend in the road he was lost to view, and so far as the prosecution were able to ascertain, was never afterwards seen alive. It appeared that Grindley, being also wishful to avoid the prisoners, went up the street towards his home at Madeley, the way to which would for a certain distance be in the same direction as that to Lawton's ... The prisoners followed in the same direction up Church Street.*

About 15 minutes later, witnesses Philip Rowley and Philip James, who had remained chatting in the street after the fracas, saw Luke and Ratcliffe running down the street from the direction of the church gates. At around the same time, a Mr Dodd who lived nearby heard a man shouting, 'murder!' several times and saw the two men running down the road. The men went into Rowley's house. Mrs Rowley – Philip's mother – didn't know Luke at all and knew Ratcliffe only by name. She later testified that the two men came in to light their pipes and stayed about 1¼ hours. She asked them to leave some time between 2.10 and 2.20 am, which of course left a gap of an hour around midnight when there was no account of their movements. Luke and Ratcliffe are then reported to have gone to the house of James Edwards, arriving at about 2.30 or 3 am. Those present testified that Ratcliffe stayed until 4.45 am, although Luke stayed until 10 am. But, there was contradictory evidence that placed the men elsewhere for at least part of the time:

Thomas Whittles, forgeman, of Silverdale said he sometimes acted as watchman for Messrs Stanier at Silverdale works and was so employed in the night in question. Any person going to the road leading from the Rompin' pit would pass the Silverdale works. In the course of the night referred to he saw Ratcliffe and another man pass. They were coming from the direction of the Rompin' pit. It was moonlight. Ratcliffe passed within 4 or 5 yards of him and he said, 'Good morning' to him. Ratcliffe made some reply that he could not understand. He could not say what time it was, but the moon had not yet gone down, and so far as he could judge it would be about 3 hours before he left work. He left work at 6 o'clock.

In other words, Whittles reckoned he'd seen them at about 3 o'clock, the time given for their arrival at James Edward's house.

There was enough gossip and knowledge for the Police to pick up John Ratcliffe, who was obviously one of the last people to have seen Cain Lawton alive on the last night for which anyone knew of his movements. William Luke, however, had left the area to live in Littleborough in Lancashire. The Police travelled to Littleborough to question him and found that his mother had been sending letters to him. She had had to dictate them to her lodger John Kent as she was illiterate. The Police found three letters in Kent's handwriting, one of which read:

Silverdale June 9 1875. Dear son – this comes with all our kind respects to you all. And I must inform you that they have found the body of Cain Lawton this morning (Wednesday) and they have found him in the Rompin engine pit. And they say he was quite naked and his clothes with him, and the boots that he had with him. And it is stated that they are going to take Ratcliffe tonight, so that you won't be surprised. They brought him up in a sheet. There is no one knows except your mother and me. If there is any disturbance we will send you word. JOHN KENT.

The evidence pointing to the two men was clear. It was reasonable to assume that they had killed Lawton at some time shortly before midnight, then spent several hours discussing what to do, before dumping his body down the Rompin Pit in the early hours of the morning.

The defence was really clutching at straws. Dr Evans, William Luke's lawyer, tried to have the Judge dismiss the case on the grounds of lack of evidence, but the Judge was having none of it. He then tried to argue that Lawton's death was an accidental suicide:

He ventured to think they would say that not only had no murder been committed but that under the circumstances of the case it was almost impossible that one could have been committed. He controverted the theory of the prosecution, and submitted another which had to be infinitely more probable. On the night in question, Cain Lawton, being drunk and having got away from his quarrelsome companions, one of whom had knocked him down and severely bruised him, felt doubtful whether he should go home that night, because it appeared from the evidence that he had said to a witness that he would stop at Silverdale. He did not wish to come in the way of these men again, and it was natural that he should go out of his ordinary road to avoid them. In such a frame of mind and under these circumstances he proceeded up by the forge and this air-shaft. He was then some considerable distance from home, he had a pair of boots in one hand and some provisions that he was carrying for a companion in the other; it was a bitterly cold night and what probably did [happen] . . . was this: he with his couple of bundles came near the air-shaft, and being too intoxicated, or knocked about, or not wishing to go home, he got over the fence, as he easily might, and on to the iron plate which was always warm from the heated air flowing up the shaft, and determined to stay there for a time. He took off his boots and prepared to sleep on that iron plate – a thing that many a man had done before him – but either from the effects of intoxication or by sheer accident, instead of continuing to lie comfortably there he fell over the edge of the plate and down the shaft.

Dr Evans also had an explanation for the fact that the clothes were found separately to the body. This might be accounted for

... by coming in contact with the scaffolding and the projecting irons in the descent. A circumstance strongly corroborative of this theory was that the wristband and part of the cuff being found on the arm. He granted that this hypothesis was an extraordinary one, but the facts were extraordinary, and there must be some way of accounting for them. He rejected the idea of the man having been first stripped naked and then thrown down the pit as incredible, and said that if men who had killed a man, and knowing the country well, had had a corpse to dispose of, it was not to be supposed that they would carry it three-quarters of a mile to put it down an air-shaft, where it was certain to be discovered, when there were numerous disused workings nearer to hand.

Mr Young, Ratcliffe's defence lawyer, further tried to poo-poo the evidence on the grounds that it had all emerged months after Lawton's disappearance.

In the event, neither lawyer had put up a convincing defence of the two men, especially given that there were possible holes and discrepancies in the witness testimony that they could have exploited. It was time for the Judge to sum up. He said that:

If the jury were of opinion that the man Lawton came by his death otherwise than at the hands of the prisoners it would be their duty to acquit them. He had hoped that the evidence would assist them to arrive at a conclusion as to how the unfortunate man came by his death, but very little light had been thrown upon the matter.

After pointing out the difference between manslaughter and murder, the learned Judge said although the evidence was circum-stantial in its character it was their duty to deal with the evidence as they found it given in that court, and it did not always follow that because evidence was circumstantial they were not to deal with it fearlessly and boldly. He then reviewed at length the evidence

given, and said that although it differed in respect of its applic-
ability to the prisoners yet if they were shown to have been acting in
concert, what was proved against the one would also affect the
other. He said it was legally open to the jury if they should think the
graver crime charged in the indictment was not established, to find
a verdict of manslaughter.

The jury took just 15 minutes to find William Luke and John
Ratcliffe guilty of manslaughter. In his sentencing, the Judge
was unable to find any redeeming feature which might recommend the prisoners to the mercy of the Court. No doubt they
had both been drinking but it was impossible to take that as an
excuse. The prisoners were each sentenced to 15 years' penal
servitude.

That the Judge left it to the jury to decide whether it was
manslaughter or murder is in many ways strange. One can only
surmise that there were enough inconsistencies in the stories of
all involved for there to be some element of doubt. Rather than
go the whole hog and dismiss the case for lack of evidence, the
jury had taken a middle path and chosen the verdict of manslaughter. On the other hand, by the standards of evidence of
the time, all too often based on hearsay, speculation and
rumour, Ratcliffe and Luke were extremely lucky not to hang.

Chapter 17

The Unkindest Cut of All
1879

Isaac, there is an open door of mercy; what is there that stands between you and it?

Victorian newspapers trod a fine line between mealy-mouthed respectability and sensationalism. One case that was to stretch the boundaries of what could be printed was that of Isaac Brooks. According to the *Staffordshire Sentinel* of 31 January 1880, what had taken place was a 'Horrible Outrage at Rushton'. The newspaper continued to give an account of the tale of:

> *Henry Johnson of Horton Hay, farmer, Samuel Clowes of the same place, farmer, and Enoch Sherratt of Biddulph, farmer, on bail, were indicted for feloniously wounding Isaac Brooks, on the 4th December 1879 with intent to do him some grievous bodily harm.*

In fact, what the *Sentinel* couldn't mention directly was that Isaac Brooks had been nearly castrated.

Clowes, Johnson and Sherratt were brought before the Stafford Assizes on 22 January 1880, a few weeks after the assault had taken place. The *Staffordshire Advertiser* of the following week reported that:

> *Mr Brindley ... the learned counsel for the prosecution, in the opening case, said that whatever opinion the jury might form on the case to be brought before them, his own was that a more dastardly and cruel act could not be committed by one man on another. He thought there might be some suggestion, on the part of the defence, that the prosecutor [i.e. Isaac Brooks], when he left the Fox Inn at Rushton, was not perfectly sober. So far as witnesses had said, and*

the lengthened cross-examination to which the prosecutor had been subjected when before the magistrates, it appeared that he had only had four or five glasses of ale. In reference to identity, the prosecutor could speak positively to Johnson and Clowes, but was not sure of Sherratt. It might assist them a little; perhaps, to know that the night of the outrage was fine, being a clear frosty, moonlight night; and this was a circumstance favourable to the prosecutor in identifying the men who attacked him.

Mr Brindley also gave a possible motive for the attack, in that Isaac Brooks had had an illegitimate child with Clowes's sister, which had caused bad blood between the two families. When he called upon Isaac Brooks to give his testimony, Brooks gave a full and detailed account, telling the court that:

On the afternoon of the 4th December he went to the Fox *Inn, at Rushton, it being rent day there, and remained until about 10 o'clock at night. At that time he left, being quite sober, in company with two men named William Knight and John Moss, and the three were soon overtaken, when going in the direction of Pyatt's Barn, by a man named Eardley. When they reached Pyatt's Barn they were overtaken by the three prisoners and a boy, whom witness had left in the* Fox *previously. They then had some whisky together. When they left Pyatt's Barn Yard, Moss and Knight left, witness and Eardley soon after left also. At a short distance beyond where he left Knight and Moss, there is a footway across the field. When they reached this one of the prisoners said they would go that way, as it was the nearest road to their homes. They continued in company until they reached the junction of the Rushton and Biddulph roads, the boy walking in front. At the corner of the Biddulph road, the prisoners went one way and witness went another, after wishing the men 'Good night'. On going along the road [he] took the money he had with him out of his right-hand trousers pocket and put it into his left-hand jacket pocket, for safety [and] went along very slowly from this point, counting his money. When he had finished, and had got about 80 yards round the curve of the road, he saw Clowes, Johnson and a man believed to be Sherratt, on the side of the road, sitting on their heels. Johnson then ran at witness, sprung on his back and pulled him down on the ground from behind and the man whom he believed to be*

Lane near Pyatt's Barn, where Isaac Brooks had been drinking with Johns, Clowes and Sherratt shortly before the 'Outrage' took place. The author

Sherratt put his hand over his mouth and a pocket handkerchief over his face. Clowes then put his hand into [Brooks's] left-hand trouser pocket and then into his right; and afterwards took down his clothes. Witness for the moment forgot the position he was in, and did not realise the same until he felt he was being cut with a knife in a tender part. Johnson and Sherratt held him some time, and with the pressure and loss of blood he became quite faint, and began to feel sick. Johnson and Sherratt then left him, and Clowes said to witness, after inflicting the horrible injury, 'Take that, you *******!' and went away. After resting some short time against a wall, [Brooks] walked slowly homewards, but found he was bleeding profusely. When he arrived home his mother attended him in the best way she could, and a doctor was sent for.

To begin with, when the doctor was called to his bedside, Brooks couldn't identify the men who had attacked him. Later he put this down to being unable to catch his breath due to pain and shock. He also told the same story to the Police. It was only some time after the attack, that he blamed Clowes, Johnson and Sherratt for his injuries. It took the Police almost a fortnight to arrest the three men and they were brought to trial on 22 January 1880.

At the trial the accused men seemed perfectly dazed and almost unable to offer any defence beyond a plain denial of the charge. There was a deal of sympathy for Brooks, whose health was obviously not particularly robust. Indeed, he testified as much in court:

Perhaps I may say that since I've had rheumatic fever I have had disease of the heart, and my medical adviser, has told me never to go into crowded assemblies, for excitement of any kind might be attended by serious consequences.

After hearing the evidence against Sherratt, the Judge instructed the jury to bring in a 'not guilty' verdict against Sherratt – as his lawyer, Mr Selfe, pointed out there was no direct evidence against him. The testimonies were mildly conflicting, but there was no doubt that Sherratt was not involved. Johnson and Clowes were not so lucky.

Mr Selfe in his address to the jury on behalf of Johnson remarked that a more mysterious as well as serious case had seldom come before a court of justice. He pointed out that the law demanded that a reasonable certainty should be brought home against a prisoner charged in a dock. That reasonable certainty, he contended, had not been established in this case, and he felt confident that when they returned their verdict, under these circumstances, it would be one of not guilty. What was the extraordinary story they were asked to believe?

He then went on to point out that there seemed no good reason why men who had been drinking companionably together should suddenly go into hiding and then jump out on their friend. He also called a variety of character witnesses, including Mr Dale, timber merchant, of Biddulph, Mr William Foster and Mr Ishmael Lancaster, farmers, also of Biddulph. Mr Brindley, the prosecutor, had already pointed out that there was bad blood between Brooks and Clowes as Clowes's sister had had an illegitimate child by Brooks. He then

> *... replied on the evidence at some length and remarked that although his learned friend, Mr Selfe, had spoken of the uncertainty which existed in this case, in point of fact, the prosecutor was positively certain of two of the men who were there on the night in question; and did they think that a man who had been held down for a considerable time, as the prosecutor had, would be unable to identify the men who not only held him but committed a horrible and gross outrage on him? He submitted that there was no reason for doubt at all; and this being so, it would be the duty of the jury to find both prisoners guilty.*

Once both sides of the argument had been given, the Judge:

> *... summed up to the jury at considerable length, entering into every detail of the case. As to motive for the outrage, regarded the same, especially of Clowes, as pretty clear; and the night on which the outrage was committed having been a bright and fine one, identity was greatly facilitated, and in his own mind there existed no doubt as regarded the case. He characterised the outrage that had been committed as a most horrible one, and remarked that the perpetrators had evidently the intention of doing the prosecutor not merely temporary but permanent injury. He trusted the jury would give the case their most serious consideration, in order to find whether the prisoners were guilty or not.*

How long it takes for a jury to give 'serious consideration' is open to conjecture. In this particular instance, the jury took all of 10 minutes to come to the conclusion that Johnson and Clowes were guilty. The Judge deferred sentencing, but eventually the two men were given 10 years' penal servitude. During this time, both men continued to protest their innocence. Indeed, Johnson made the following written declaration on 23 February 1880:

> *To my trustees Messrs William Corbishley and John Corbishley, of Horton, near Leek, farmers, and to my solicitor, Mr Frederick Greatrex, of Stafford, and to all other persons whom it may concern: I do hereby instruct and authorise you and each of you to*

use every possible endeavour to obtain a remission of my sentence of 10 years penal servitude, as I most solemnly declare that I am innocent of the charge upon which I was convicted at the assizes held at Stafford in January last, and with this view I hereby retain and engage the services of my solicitor, Mr Frederick Greatrex, of Stafford, to thoroughly investigate the circumstances connected with the charge upon which I was indicted, and to petition the Home Secretary and do all the things necessary on my behalf. And I hereby empower and authorise my trustees, Messrs Wm Corbishley and John Corbishley to retain and pay all costs, charges and expenses which shall be incurred by them and my said solicitor out of my trust estate and property.

However, while Johnson and Clowes were both serving their sentences, Isaac Brooks was again attacked. Dr Warrington revealed:

I was sent for again to see Isaac Brooks on the 13th February 1881. On arriving at his bedside about 4 p.m. and upon asking him what was the matter he answered, 'I have the same complaint, I had more than a year ago.' I said, 'What was that – rheumatism?' He said, 'No, I've been again attacked on the same road, but higher up, by four men. I tried to escape, and had nearly done so by getting over a wall, but they caught me, unfastened my trousers and hurt me.' It occurred about 11.30 the night before. After describing the injuries Dr Warrington proceeds – 'There had been extensive haemorrhage. Cobwebs, tobacco, dry rags etc. had been applied to stop the haemorrhaging. He informed me that after the outrage on him he applied his pocket handkerchief to the wound, which at that time bled freely, and walked home. During the night, after he had got very warm in bed and gone to sleep, the bleeding commenced again, and he awoke, finding the bed saturated with blood and running on the floor. He called up his mother, being greatly alarmed, and after applying the above mentioned remedies, the bleeding still continuing, a large hairpin was thrust through the tissues from where the blood came, and round this was twisted a quantity of worsted. This, he informed me, for the time being answered effectively the intended purpose. After giving him what instructions I thought necessary, I left him.

So, were the men correct to have protested their innocence, or was someone wreaking revenge for Brooks' having sent them to gaol? To be attacked in the same way twice was almost beyond belief.

The truth was to emerge a few months later in a bizarre twist that was carried by the *Staffordshire Advertiser* of 7 and 14 January 1882. After recapping the story of Isaac Brooks so far, the newspaper went on to report a visit to a dying Isaac Brooks by Mr Harrison, a local Wesleyan preacher:

> ... *his notion being that the sick man wanted to talk to him about business matters. However, he remained by his bedside, or in the house, 7 hours before Brooks approached the subject of the crime, and the conversation was almost entirely religious. He spoke to me, Mr Harrison said on god's faithfulness and promises, and betwixt 12.00 and 2.00 in the morning he became restless and disturbed, and said he doubted whether he should not be lost. I said, 'Isaac, there is an open door of mercy; what is there that stands between you and it?' He said, 'Nothing but unbelief.' That remark he repeated twice. The conversation was prior to the confession.*
>
> *The following conversation then took place.*
> *Brooks: 'Harrison, I can't die till I have confessed.'*
> *Harrison: 'Confessed what?'*
> *Brooks: 'That those two men are innocent.'*
> *Harrison: 'What Johnson & Clowes?'*
> *Brooks: 'Yes; but do not tell anyone till after I am dead.'*
> *Harrison: 'But Isaac, my bare word will be a very little thing. Let me write it down and you sign it.'*
>
> *Brooks: 'Yes, that will be best.' Brooks then dictated the following confession: 'December 31 1881. I Isaac Brooks, do confess that both the men, Henry Johnson and Samuel Clowes, are innocent of the crime for which I transported them, and my wish is that they shall be liberated.' The document was then signed in the presence of Harrison and Brooks's mother, who by this time had awakened. Harrison then called up Brooks's brother, and in spite of the opposition of Brooks, who did not wish his mother to know until after his death, read the confession aloud. Harrison then asked Brooks if the statement was right, to which Brooks replied in the affirmative, the mother exclaiming, 'Oh, God, what shall I do?' A*

few minutes afterwards, Brooks, who appeared greatly relieved by what he had testified, said, 'I should not have done it myself if I had not been persuaded.' Brooks died a few hours afterwards.

So, Johnson and Clowes were innocent and had been convicted on Brooks's perjured testimony. As the nineteenth century local historian, Mr W. Payne points out:

The confession ... was forwarded to the Home Secretary, an inquiry was instituted, and a gross miscarriage of justice being shown to have been committed, the 'crimeless criminals' were released. Mr Y W Craig, the MP for North Staffordshire, took a deep interest in their case, and mainly through his instrumentality they were each awarded £500 by the Government as compensation for their sufferings.

And so Johnson and Clowes returned to their lives £500 (over £30,000 in today's money) better off. But neither man was as robust as he had been before spending 2 years on a prison ship at Chatham.

This is not the only self-inflicted injury that was initially reported as an assault to be recorded in the annals of Staffordshire crime. On 6 April 1813, the following notice went up under the heading 'Robbery and Murder':

Whereas last Night about Half past Seven o'clock, as Mr RALPH BOWERS, of the Dolphin, in Shelton, was returning home from the Lane Delph, across the Fields, he was stopped by Three Footpads, at Botteslow Green, who robbed him of FIVE POUNDS, one TWO POUNDS and one ONE POUND Bank of England Notes, and afterwards attempted to murder him by cutting his Throat in several places: Notice is hereby given, that whoever will give such information as may lead to the discovery of the Perpetrators of the above atrocious deed, shall receive a handsome Reward: and if either of the persons concerned in the Robbery will impeach his Accomplices, he will be well rewarded, and have every means used to obtain a pardon.

One of the Robbers was a tall, stout Man, in a Fustian Jacket: the others were rather short, and dressed in Flannel Jackets; and from their appearance, are supposed to be Colliers. Three Men answering the above description, were seen going from Hanley towards Botteslow about Seven o'clock last Night.

A Razor was found early this Morning, on the Spot where the Robbery was committed, rather rusty and stained with blood: with a curved black Haft; and stamped on the Blade, 'Marriot, Warranted'.

Even though Bowers gave a full description of the men, they were never found. They were never likely to be either. In an interesting appendix to the case, the Staffordshire pottery manufacturer, Enoch Wood, who collected all sorts of ephemera and notices and whose collection is now part of the Stoke-on-Trent city archives added a note to the notice in his handwriting declaring that the local authorities had 'found it was his [Bower's] own act'.

In those days, suicide was a crime and poor Mr Bowers had probably attempted to take his own life and, after several attempts to cut his own throat, given up. However, he would have needed an explanation for his wounds and creating a story based on an attack by footpads would have seemed as good an excuse as any.

As to what led Isaac Brooks to mutilate himself, we can only speculate. It was a strange act, and one for which he needed a scapegoat. In the end, he found two – Johnson and Clowes.

CHAPTER 18

Murder and Suicide at the *Falcon Inn*
1891

The upper and lower jaws were blown away – in fact the whole front of the face – not a feature being left.

In the late nineteenth century, the small market town of Stone was a quiet, respectable place – not the kind of spot you'd expect to come across a double shooting. But on the evening of 17 February 1891, two shots rang out that both shocked the residents and left them with enough gossip for decades to come.

It was at 10.25 pm that William Strefford, the manager of the *Falcon Inn* at the bottom of Stone High Street, sent for his wife Mary to join him in the vaults. While waiting for her, he took hold of a double-barrelled gun and angled it across the counter. When his wife arrived, he pulled the trigger. A few minutes later, a second shot rang out. Strefford had placed the gun vertically under his own chin and pulled the trigger.

There was no one else in the vaults at the time. William's sister, who had been working as a maid for the couple, had been to fetch Mary on William's orders. Two customers, a Mr Shardlow and a Mr Flowers, were elsewhere in the pub and didn't react immediately to the first shot, realising there was something wrong only when they heard the second. The *Staffordshire Advertiser* of 21 February takes up the story:

A young man named Charles Flowers went down to see what had happened and was horrified on opening the door of the vaults, to see Mrs Strefford lying on the floor in a pool of blood. The door opens to the left, and Flowers waited to see no more but summoned help, and

Joseph Shardlow, who was also in the bar, and Eugene Turner came in. The last named went for the Police, while Shardlow and others remained at the door to keep people away.

A large crowd soon assembled, and on arrival of Police-Sergt Draper and a constable at 10.30pm the whole facts were evident. On opening the door the officer found both Strefford and his wife dead on the floor outside the counter.

Strefford's face, indeed the front part of his head, was blown away, as if a rough vertical section of it had been made from the

The Falcon Inn, *Stone. The location of the murder and suicide of Mary and* William Strefford, *currently a restaurant.* The author

prominent part of the larynx to the roof of the skull; while the whole
of the lower jaw of the unfortunate woman to the centre of the base of
the skull was also blown away, the ceiling, the walls, the gas shades,
and the counter were bespattered with the blood and the brains of the
unfortunate and unhappy couple, and so close had the charges been
fired that not a shot seems to have gone wide of its mark, the glasses,
mirror, gas-shades and everything being undamaged. The bodies
lay feet to feet, and a double-barrelled breech-loading gun was lying
on the floor between them. The woman's left hand was clenched
and raised towards her head, and from the position of the bodies it
would seem that Strefford waited at the end of the vaults to the left of
the door – the space between the counter and the outer wall being
only narrow and some 10 or 12 yards long – and shot his wife soon
after she had entered. The position of her hand would argue that
she had seized the muzzle of the gun and that it was close to her left
jaw when it was discharged, pointing from the left in an upward
direction. The whole of the charge, therefore, was delivered into the
unfortunate woman's head. Strefford, after this, would seem to
have stood at the feet of his wife and fired upwards at himself –
in fact leaned with his head over the muzzle of the gun and fired.
The gun was a breech-loading one and a 12-bore. Strefford kept it
in a little recess at the end of the vaults behind the bar and was in
the habit of filling his own cartridges, having purchased a fresh
supply of powder, shot and wads about 3 weeks ago. The gun was
lying on the right side of the woman, her right heel resting on the
muzzle. Both bodies were quite warm when Police-Sergeant
Draper arrived at 10.30 but the sight was almost too horrible to
witness. Death must have been instantaneous in both cases. The
bodies were removed across the yard into an outhouse and laid side
by side. The man was a dark, good-looking fellow, about 5ft 8in.
tall and his wife was tall for a woman and approaching 5ft 6in.
In the house, beside themselves, were a young man, who helped
generally and Mr Strefford's sister a young woman about 18 years
old, who had had a terrible experience and has since been
prostrated with grief.

This was Strefford's poor 18-year-old sister Jane, who was
living and working at the *Falcon Inn,* and who had to identify
the two bodies. There was gossip that she'd been invited to

work for them not by her brother, but by Mary, who thought that she would help keep the peace. It was no pleasant sight for Mary, for at the inquest, Horace Hartley, medical practitioner at Stone

> ... *described the wounds of the woman as follows: 'A lacerated wound involving the larynx, trachea, lower jaw and floor of the mouth and tongue, and the main vessels of the side of the neck, the carotid arteries and jugular veins. The wound was evidently caused by gunshots. Death must have been instantaneous and the gun discharged quite close to her.' In the case of the man he said, 'The upper and lower jaws were blown away – in fact the whole front of the face – not a feature being left. The muzzle of the gun must have been put to the chin and discharged by the foot. Death, of course, was instantaneous. The injury to the man must have been self-inflicted, and the shot must have been fired directly upwards. With regard to the wife, the gun must have been pointed obliquely and she must have been standing with her face half turned, towards her husband.*

The death of the Streffords was a complete shock. Little was known about them in the town. Neither William nor Mary was local. William was a Shropshire lad and Mary had been born in Liverpool as Ada Mary Berks. They had not been in the town very long and, during that time, they had suffered the tragedy of their young daughter's death. Gossip was rife. It held that William Strefford was often abusive to his wife, threatening her with his fists, and a few days before the killing had even stabbed her in the shoulder with a knife. There were also rumours of infidelity. The newspaper report stated that:

> *The couple have not lived very happily together, and though they have a little boy upwards of 4 years old, who lives with his grand-parents near Wellington, the loss of a 4½ months infant in December seems to have preyed unduly on the unfortunate man's mind. So much was this the case that in early January he went out one evening to the grave, and remaining so long, his wife, with a woman named Byatt, went to seek him. They found him at midnight lying on the child's grave. He had scraped the snow from it, and his mind was certainly unhinged. The carpenter,*

Jenkinson, who made the coffin for the little one, adds that Strefford on the evening of the murder said to him on entering the vaults on the occasion referred to above. 'You made my little boy's coffin, and I shall soon have another job for you,' or words to that effect.

Jenkinson put the coffin remark down as being a piece of pub-banter. However, while there had been some indications of tension and violence between the two, nobody could have expected the outburst of extreme violence that ended the Streffords' lives:

During the day Strefford had been apparently in his sober senses, though, as we have said, suffering from the effects of drinking. So much was this the case, that feeling unwell he went to Mr Jenkins, the chemist's shop, on the night of the tragedy for some medicine, having bought some pills there on Monday night. This was between 6 and 7 o'clock and here Mr Jenkins said he seemed a little excited. Mr Jenkins gave him a bottle of aperient medicine and told him he had been drinking too much. The deceased said he would leave off drinking and added that he had had nothing all day except some champagne in the morning. A man who knew him well said he asked Strefford what was the matter with him in the afternoon, and told him he looked as if he had been crying. Strefford replied, 'everyone tells me that,' and clenching his teeth added, 'I shall be alright directly.'

Inquests into deaths were often held in public houses at the time, so it was convenient that the deaths had taken place in the *Falcon Inn*, for that was exactly where the inquest into the Strefford's deaths was held. Much of the gossip about the couple came to light. When asked if the couple quarrelled, Jane Strefford testified that:

They did quarrel on Saturday night between 11.00 and 12.00, and when in the bedroom he tried to stab his wife with a dagger that he had bought among some other things to place in the bedroom. The deceased woman, witness added, was jealous of her husband. Witness stopped him when he attacked his wife. It was the only time the witness had seen her brother attack his wife. Her sister-in-law had attempted to cut her throat, and witness had prevented her about 3 weeks ago. This was in consequence of some quarrel. On the Saturday night when he attempted to stab his wife, the latter had been drinking.

Jane Strefford also told the inquest that:

On the night of the tragedy both of them were sober. The loss of his child in December seemed to have had a depressing effect upon him and he had been strange ever since, but had not taken any more to drink. He continually visited the grave of the child, and was found there one night after 12 o'clock.

John Holmes, the barman testified that the Streffords were both sober on the night. He seemed surprised by the events, although a clue to what was to happen was given by Eugene Turner, a grocer who lived opposite the *Falcon Inn*. According to the report of the inquest:

*He had seen Strefford in the morning of Tuesday. He was then wild in appearance and flushed. He was sober but appeared both ill and as if he had been drinking. Witness told Strefford that he had the 'blues' and advised him to get some Liebig's extract of beef, and added that a glass of champagne would do him good. Strefford also said that he felt very ill and 'worritted', and when witness said he had nothing to 'worrit' him, Strefford answered, 'I have, that ******* wife of mine is so very jealous, I cannot live for her.' They did not get on very well together, but witness had not seen them quarrel. By the Foreman: Strefford said also on the same occasion, 'That ******* wife of mine, she is not fit to live.'*

But like Jenkinson and the joke about the coffin, Holmes dismissed this as mere talk.

In reality, nobody seemed to know a great deal. There were tales that Strefford had had an abscess removed from his head as a boy and that this might have had an effect on his behaviour. At best we can say that the inquest pieced together a mixture of jealousy, grief, domestic abuse and alcohol that provided the impetus for William Strefford to reach such levels of despair.

The Coroner, in summing up, pointed out there was little or no doubt how the crime had been committed in the case of the wife. With regard to the man, it would be their duty to consider the state of mind in which he was at the time he destroyed himself. Without retiring, the jury decided that: 'Strefford murdered his wife and then committed suicide, being of unsound mind at the time.'

In keeping with the quiet respectability of the town, William and Mary Strefford were buried by the Rev. Johnson in St Michael's churchyard in Stone. The inscriptions on their tomb revealed nothing of the violence of the two deaths, simply giving the couple's names, ages and dates of death. While the Rector might have been trying for a quiet funeral, a small market town is still full of people who want to know what's going on. By all accounts the funeral route from the *Falcon Inn* to St Michael's Church was packed with gawping onlookers. They would gawp several times over the next few years, as this was the first in a series of three murders in a period of 8 years.

In January 1897, there was another murder and suicide. In this case, a young unmarried woman, who had once been a housemaid to the composer Edward Elgar, gave birth to an

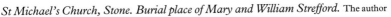

St Michael's Church, Stone. Burial place of Mary and William Strefford. The author

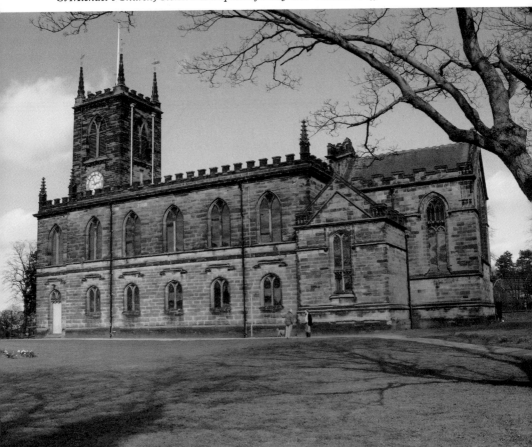

illegitimate child at a house in Oulton Road, Stone. The child was probably that of the son of the house, Henry Shingler, who lived with his mother at that address. Evidently, buying a gun in Stone was easy in those days, as Shingler did so claiming he was going to America and would need it for self-defence. As it was, he shot the baby's mother, Annie Hines, and then himself. Annie seems to have died instantly, not so Henry Shingler, who lingered on for several days before dying of his wounds in hospital in Stafford.

Then, just 2 years later – as killing one's partner was becoming something of a fashion in Stone – a man by the name of James Flower, wearing bloodstained clothing, was found wandering up and down the High Street by a local Policeman. Flower collared the officer and told him, 'I have killed the Missus.' He led the Policeman back to his house in Newcastle Road and, sure enough, while the children had remained untouched, his wife had been savagely attacked with a knife and was dead. Flower had been complaining of headaches and dizziness for some time and had started drinking heavily as a

Oulton Road, Stone. The house is no longer standing, where Henry Shingler killed his girlfriend and himself in a bizarre repeat of the Strefford case of six years earlier.
The author

Newcastle Road, Stone. It was here that James Flower murdered his wife. The author

way of relieving the pain (although of course, alcohol consumption was more likely to aggravate these symptoms than cure them). He was found guilty of murder, but held not to be responsible for his actions. Flower was committed to an asylum for the rest of his life.

CHAPTER 19

The Real Sherlock Holmes Investigates
1903

The first sight which I ever had of Mr George Edalji was enough ... to convince me ... of the extreme improbability of his being guilty of the crime for which he was condemned ...

S ir Arthur Conan Doyle is of course best known as the creator of Sherlock Holmes, the fictional detective who used logic and deductive reasoning to solve crimes. However, in his later years, Conan Doyle began applying some of the techniques used by his fictional character to investigate real-life crimes himself. He recounted some of these escapades in his 1924 book, *Memories and Adventures*, including that of his involvement in the case of a young man named George Edalji:

> *It was late in 1906 that I chanced to pick up a paper called 'The Umpire' and my eye caught an article which was a statement of his [George Edalji's] case, made by himself, though how he smuggled it out of prison I know not ... As I read, the unmistakable force of the truth fixed itself on my attention and I realised that I was in the presence of an appalling tragedy, and that I was called upon to do what I might to set it right.*

George Edalji was a Birmingham lawyer, educated at Rugeley Grammar School and Mason College in Birmingham (later to become Birmingham University), before being articled as a clerk to Messrs. King and Ludlow in Birmingham. He was an

Rugeley Grammar School. An artist's impression of Rugeley Grammar School after a drawing by John Buckler (around 1824). Both William Palmer and George Edalji attended Rugeley Grammar School. The author

excellent scholar and had won Law Society prizes, even penning a book on the subject of railway law. He was a teetotal non-smoker. His father, Shapurji Edalji, was a vicar and the author of several books, which had helped to fund his passage to England and his training for the priesthood. His mother was the daughter (and niece) of an Anglican clergyman. In every way, George was the archetypal scion of the British middle-classes. Every way, that is, except one: for, in the language of the day, George was 'half-caste' – his father being Indian and his mother, Charlotte Stoneham, a white British woman.

George Edalji's story, one of wrongful arrest and imprisonment, soon had Conan Doyle on the trail of justice. Not only was Doyle able to clear George's name, but he was also able to identify whom he thought a much more likely candidate for the crimes of which George had been accused.

In and around the village of Great Wyrley, at the turn of the twentieth century, there had been a series of bizarre, sinister, seemingly motiveless attacks on animals. Several horses, cows and sheep were slashed with some kind of sharp knife and then left to die where they lay. A sick mind was at work and Police were at a loss as to who the culprit could be. Then they began receiving letters relating to the crime. Some were unsigned, others bore the name of a boy called Wilfred Greatorex, a pupil at Walsall Grammar School, although he was quickly proven not to be the sender. If the crimes were bizarre, so was the content of the letters, which gloated over the deeds and boasted of the gang that was involved, mentioning several of the residents of Great Wyrley by name. A letter dated 10 July 1903 declared that: 'there will be merry times in Wyrley in November when they start on little girls, for they will do twenty wenches like the horse before next March.'

Then, on the morning of 18 August, a horse was found attacked, but still alive in a field that provided a short-cut to the

St Mark's Church, Great Wyrley. George Edalji's father was the vicar at the time of George's arrest. The author

nearby colliery. The colliery vet was called, but the horse proved too ill to save and had to be put down.

The letters had predicted the crime and, although the Police were out in force that night, no-one had spotted the perpetrator. The nearest house was the vicarage, ½ mile or so away across open land and, even before 8 o'clock that morning, the Police had raided the house and taken away a pair of boots and a razor belonging to the vicar's son, who was later arrested. According to the Reverend Edalji's statement:

> *As soon as they [the Police] saw the old coat they began to examine it, and Inspector Campbell put his finger upon one of the stains and said that there was a hair there. Mrs Edalji told him that it was not a hair but a thread, and Miss Edalji, who was present, then remarked that it looked like a 'roving' [a loose thread]. This was all that inspector Campbell had said to them about hairs before I came down. When I saw him he told me that he had found horse hairs upon the coat. The coat was then spread out upon the desk in the study. I asked him to point out the places where the hairs were to be seen. He pointed out the lower part of the coat and said, 'There is a horsehair there.' I examined the place and said, 'There is no hair here at all.' Some further conversation followed, and then suddenly he put his finger upon another place on the coat nearer to where I was standing and drew two straight lines with his finger. He said, 'Look here, Mr Edalji, there is horsehair here.' I looked at the place for a moment, and in order to have more light upon it, I took up the coat with both my hands and drew nearer to the window, and after carefully examining it, I said to him, 'There is, to be sure, no horsehair here. It is a clean surface.' He then said that he wanted to take the coat with him, and I said, 'You can take the coat. I am satisfied there is no horsehair upon it.' Now, I have said it over and over again, and I say it here once more, that there was absolutely no horsehair upon the coat. If there had been any, I could not have failed to see it, and Mrs Edalji and Miss Edalji looked at the coat at the same time and saw no hair of any sort upon it.*

Inspector Campbell, however, had a different view of events. His evidence in the Police Court, Cannock, 19 August 1903 is revealing. According to the records:

He found in the inner side of both cuffs of the jacket a dark reddish stain. The one on the right cuff was 4 inches long by a ½ inch wide at the widest part, which had the appearance of partly dried blood. On the left cuff was a similar stain, but not quite so bad. On both sleeves there were numerous stains of a whitish colour, which had the appearance of saliva.

On both cuffs of the jacket he found brownish coloured hairs, which seem to be those belonging to a horse. There were other hairs on the breast of the jacket, which was damp . . . On the left breast of the waistcoat there were several horse hairs, similar to those found on the jacket.

By 11 o'clock of the morning of the attack, Police arrested George at his office in Birmingham: 'I have been expecting this for some time,' said George as he was led away: words later interpreted as a sure sign of guilt. There is, however, a much more likely explanation. George was already well-known to the Police. The family had been at the centre of what would nowadays be described as a 'hate campaign'. In 1888, obscene graffiti about the family was scrawled on walls in Great Wyrley. A young girl by the name of Elizabeth Foster had worked as a maid for the Edaljis and for some reason bore a grudge against them – perhaps the idea of a white girl being employed by a man with dark skin was too much for her. She was taken to court over the offences, found guilty and bound over to keep the peace. The hounding of the Edaljis had stopped – at least for a while. Then, between 1892 and 1895, hate mail began arriving at the vicarage. The Reverend Edalji reported the matter to the local Police. There were also other bizarre incidents: other vicars received letters purporting to be from Shapurji Edalji; and the key to the door of Walsall Grammar School was reported stolen, then found on the steps of the Great Wyrley Vicarage. An advert appeared in the *Blackpool Times* in December 1895:

WANTED, immediately lady or gentleman to adopt an Orphan Girl aged 7, handsome and remarkably intelligent . . . £100 paid down to suitable person. For full particulars and explanation Rev. S Edalji, Great Wyrley, Walsall.

The Chief Constable, Captain the Honourable George Augustus Anson, was certain that George was the perpetrator. During the outbreak of vandalism, petty crime and letter-writing, he had in fact written to Shapurji Edalji to say he thought that George was the writer of the letters and wrote: 'I may say at once that I shall not pretend to believe any protestations of ignorance which your son may make about the key [to Walsall Grammar School].'

Following his arrest, as he served his time in custody, George explained to the Police that he was quite happy to be there. The horse-slasher would strike again while he was in the cells, thereby proving his innocence. If he was there, then that would be the greatest alibi of all – there would be no way he could be involved in the next crime. Sure enough, while he was awaiting trial, there was a further attack. The *Illustrated Mail*, 10 October 1903, carries the story:

> *On the morning of September 22, a miner on his way to work, when about 5 minutes' walk from the vicarage where the parents of the accused man [George Edalji] reside, found a valuable charger worth £50 belonging to Mr Harry Green, a member of the Walsall troop of Yeomanry, lying dead with a horrible wound across its abdomen. The poor animal had evidently galloped about a good deal before it finally fell down to die. Last week Mr Green received a letter stating that all his horses are marked out by the 'gang' to be killed. A young woman of Great Wyrley has also received a threatening letter . . . .*
>
> *A public meeting was held last week at Great Wyrley to discuss the crimes and decide on future action, and it was agreed to send a memorandum to the Home Secretary appealing to him to give all the expert assistance he could in order if possible to trace the offender and to protect the village from further outrage. It is estimated that the value of the animals which have been killed amounts to £450, and a fund has been started to compensate the owners.*
>
> *The Staffordshire Police are now in possession of information throwing considerable light upon the strange series of cattle-maiming outrages in the parish of Great Wyrley.*
>
> *They have received an explanation, having something of the*

nature of a confession, bearing upon the last outrage on September 21. This is believed to have the effect of entirely dissociating it from the earlier cases, in respect of which the young Birmingham solicitor Edalji is awaiting trial.

At the end of the piece came this short sentence, which spelled devastating news for George Edalji: 'It is not expected that any arrests will follow.'

Why should there be arrests? To the Police, this crime while he was locked up didn't prove George's innocence, but simply showed that he was part of a larger gang. The Police had their man. In fact, they now had the entire Great Wyrley Gang, as they also arrested a young lad called Harry Green, son of the horse's owner, who signed a confession for the horse killing of 21 September, so the matter was at an end.

In fact, Green was waiting for a ticket of passage to South Africa, and once he had it, claimed the confession had been bullied out of him. Given there were two further attacks later that year, for which neither man could have been responsible – George was in gaol and Harry out of the country – there might have been grounds for pronouncing their innocence. But at his trial, despite the flimsiness of the evidence, George Edalji was found guilty and sentenced to 7 years' hard labour. One cannot imagine the frail, bookish, effete, near-blind George Edalji, with his soft office worker's hands, taking easily to prison life. But he battled through 3 years of his sentence, before being unexpectedly released.

He was no longer able to practice law, having been struck off the register, but worked as a legal clerk instead, which indicates not only George's willingness to rebuild something of his life, but an act of faith on the part of the firm of solicitors, in taking on someone who had been gaoled in such a high-profile case. In fact, during his time in gaol, 10,000 people signed a petition on George's behalf, including many lawyers. His mother wrote letters drumming up support, including the following defence of George:

Our son always lived at home, going each day either to School, College, or Office, only being absent at night when away for short visits or to London for his examinations. He was always kind and

St Mark's Church, Great Wyrley with the former vicarage, where George Edalji lived while working as a solicitor in Birmingham. The author

> *dutiful to us, and from a child was always kind to any dumb creature; it would have been quite impossible for him to maim, or injure, any animal; and my husband, daughter, servant and I, who were the only people besides our son who were in the house on the night of the 17th August 1903, are quite sure he never left the house from 9.27 p.m. on the 17th to 7.55 a.m. on the 18th when he left to go by his usual train to his office in Birmingham. Our son was of a very studious nature, as may be known for the numerous Prizes he took from Law classes &c. and from passing the Final Examination and taking 2nd class Honours. He is also the author of* Railway Law for the Man in the Train, *one of Wilson's Legal Handy books.*

It was around this time the case came to Conan Doyle's attention. He looked over the evidence placed before the original jury and found it lacking in substance. For a start, George shared a room with his father, who swore that he had not left the house the previous night. Indeed, the only time George had left the house was earlier in the day, when he went to have his shoes repaired – well before the attack could possibly have taken place – and this was confirmed by two alibi witnesses. However, Conan Doyle was looking for something more concrete. The Police had refused to believe George hadn't sent himself his own hate mail, so why should alibi evidence be upheld? He decided to stick to some material facts and challenged the evidence on four further counts.

First, he reckoned that George's myopia made him an unlikely culprit. Writing in the *Daily Telegraph* in 1907, Conan Doyle stated that:

> *The first sight which I ever had of Mr George Edalji was enough . . . to convince me . . . of the extreme improbability of his being guilty of the crime for which he was condemned and to suggest some at least of the reasons which had led to his being suspected. He had come to my hotel by appointment but I had been delayed, and he was passing the time by reading the paper . . . He held the paper close to his eyes and rather sideways, proving not only a high degree of myopia, but marked astigmatism. The idea of such a man scouring fields at night and assaulting cattle while avoiding the watching Police was ludicrous to anyone who can imagine what the world looks like to eyes with myopia of eight dioptres.*

Second, the footprint evidence seemed entirely flimsy. There were so many people milling around the scene of the horse's attack that the boot prints used as evidence against George could have been almost anyone's. Given the fact that the field was also a short-cut to the mine, the idea of matching the print became even more ludicrous. Mud on George's trousers did not even match the mud in the field, but bore out the story of visiting the village boot-maker, John Hands. In fact, the evidence of the Police Constable, cross-examined in the original trial, should have been dismissed out-of-hand. The trial records reveal the following cross-examination:

> *'Were these footprints photographed?'*
> *'No, sir.'*

'*Was a cast made of them?*'

'*No, sir.*'

'*Then where is the evidence? Why didn't you dig up a clod of earth, so as to get a perfect impression?*'

'*Well, sir, the ground was too soft in one place and too hard in another.*'

'*But how did you measure the footprints?*'

'*With bits of stick, sir, and a straw.*'

Third was the evidence concerning the horse-hairs on George's coat. The coat with hairs was not the one worn by George on the night that the attack was supposed to have taken place. Moreover, if there weren't any hairs on the jacket while in the house, there was a clear explanation for why they might have been on it by the time it got to the Police Station. The officers simply stuffed it into the same bag that already contained a sample of the hide of the unfortunate horse that had been slashed during the night.

Finally, Conan Doyle was certain that the shaving razor that was supposed to be George's weapon of choice wasn't up to the task and that the perpetrator would have needed something more substantial.

By May of 1907, the commission set up to reinvestigate the Edalji case (in the days before the right of appeal) had reported to the Home Secretary, who granted Edalji a free pardon. However, the committee failed to award George any compensation, because it maintained he had sent the anonymous letters to himself, thus being at least partly instrumental in his own downfall. This may seem strange. After all, the only person who had ever maintained George had sent the letters was the Chief Constable of Staffordshire, Captain the Honourable George Anson (and consequently the Police Officers who served under him). Might this have been a face-saving gesture? Coincidentally, one of the three judges on the commission was Sir Albert de Rutzen, Captain Anson's cousin.

Conan Doyle was still not satisfied. He was convinced George had not sent those letters, so he set about trying to work out who might: eventually coming to believe that two letter-writers were involved. What puzzled Conan Doyle was, if

George was sending the letters, why did they stop for such a long period? Between 1895 and 1903, there had been no letters at all. Surely, if George was simply trying to attract attention to himself, he'd have continued to write letters? His resulting detective work suggested a much more likely candidate for the crimes. Conan Doyle examined the letters in detail, in the same manner his fictional detective Sherlock Holmes would have done, looking for links between them, and for any recurring themes. He noticed that there seemed to be some sort of connection with Walsall Grammar School: for example, there was the business of the school key being found on the vicarage doorstep. Doyle wondered if there might have been a pupil at the school who stood out as a possible source for the letters.

He got in touch with the Headmaster of the school, who identified immediately one boy, Royden Sharp, who had consistently performed badly at school and been a disruptive element. On at least one occasion, Sharp had been reported for slashing seats on the train on the way to school. He had also been away on a cattle-boat for a period, which coincided with the gap between the two series of letters. Despite his proven innocence, and the fact that Conan Doyle had even supplied the name of a potential culprit, George Edalji was never compensated for his wrongful conviction or his loss of earnings while in prison.

There is little doubt that racial prejudice played its part in the conviction of George Edalji. Under normal circumstances, it would be usual to believe an Anglican priest, yet Edalji's alibi for his son was dismissed. One must also have severe doubts about the level of racial tolerance of Captain the Honourable George Anson, the Chief Constable of Staffordshire, and the fact that he was cousin to Sir Albert de Rutzen, who was on the commission that reinvestigated the Edalji case. In his book, *The Real World of Sherlock Holmes*, Peter Costello is convinced the appearance of a 'coloured' vicar with a white wife in a rural parish was bound to raise suspicion: 'It was,' he writes, 'after all the duty of the English to evangelise the Blacks, not the Blacks to preach to the English.' Conan Doyle, however, kept faith in a young man whom he saw as the British Dreyfus. At no point did Conan Doyle doubt that George had been the victim of intolerable racial prejudice, and an establishment that closed ranks to prevent itself from being accused of bigotry, miscarriage of justice and lack of transparency.

As for Conan Doyle, he had worked tirelessly on the case. As Compton Mackenzie, the author of *Whisky Galore*, commented: 'Conan Doyle worked on Edalji's case from December 1906 to the following August. During that time he did no work of his own. He paid all the expenses involved.' It was a hugely generous gesture. When the widowed Conan Doyle married his second wife, Jean Leckie in 1907, Edalji was the guest of honour.

The *Daily Telegraph* organised a collection on George's behalf, raising around £300 for him (over £20,000 in today's money). George was restored to the roll of solicitors in 1907 and went on to practice law in London. He died in Hertfordshire in 1953, aged 85. In keeping with great literary tradition, the story of Conan Doyle and George Edalji was given a fictional reworking by Julian Barnes in his novel *Arthur and George*.

As a coda to the story, in 1934, the authorities made an arrest that may help to clear up the matter of Conan Doyle's second letter-writer. In November 1934 *The Times* printed the following story under the headline, 'Labourer sent to penal servitude':

Enoch Knowles, aged 57, a Darlaston labourer, was sentenced at the Stafford Assizes yesterday to 3 years' penal servitude for sending menacing and obscene letters through the post.

There were several charges against Knowles in relation to letters to women, the letters usually being dispatched after they had given evidence in the Courts in various cases. It was alleged that they contained threats to kill and were filthy in tone.

Mr A.J. Long, who prosecuted, said that Judges and a journalist, among others, had been threatened with violence, and in one case, when writing to a woman, Knowles described himself as 'Jack the Ripper of Whitechapel'.

The case had now let light on some things that had worried the authorities in the county for some years. In 1903, when Knowles was only 26 years of age, there was a case at the Quarter Sessions at

Shire Hall, Stafford. There have been various civic buildings on this site, but the Shire Hall dates from the end of the eighteenth century. It was used as a court of law until the 1990s. The author

Stafford of a man tried for maiming horses at Great Wyrley. The case attracted wide interest. The accused man was sentenced to 7 years' penal servitude, but later was granted a pardon. He [the Counsel] was not suggesting that the Home Secretary was affected in any way by the letters Knowles wrote.

Following the trial all sorts of people who had been connected with the case got letters, and the letters indicated that in spite of the conviction the maimings would go on. Letters were received giving the times and places where maimings would take place. Most of the letters purported to come from a person who signed himself 'Darby, Captain of the Wyrley Gang'.

CHAPTER 20

Thomas Gaskin and the Headless Woman
1919

The manner in which he killed her, and the efforts he made afterwards to conceal his crime by cutting up her body, are so full of ferocious, inhuman details that it is a task that I shudder at having to present to any jury in the court.

When a woman is killed or disappears, the first person to come under suspicion is the husband. So it was with Thomas Gaskin. He and his young wife Elizabeth were living apart. She had gone to live with her mother, a Mrs Talbot, at Brindley Heath, near Hednesford. On Wednesday 19 February 1919, a note arrived. On it were the words, 'Meet me round the pool at once – important.' The note was in Thomas's handwriting and had been delivered by a friend of Thomas Gaskin's, Tom Saunders. Both men worked at the nearby West Cannock Colliery.

Elizabeth left her mother in charge of her young baby and promptly went out to meet Thomas. The pool in question was situated nearby, close to the offices of the Cannock and Rugeley Colliery. She should have been back within a couple of hours. When she didn't return, her mother notified the Police. They began trying to piece together Elizabeth's movements on the day she had disappeared. Next day, Thomas Gaskin was questioned by Police. He denied having met his wife, but two officials from the colliery stated they'd seen Thomas and Elizabeth walking past the offices towards the woods, and that the couple appeared to be arguing. They saw the couple part and leave in opposite directions.

Elizabeth had been alive when last seen and Thomas walking away from her: if he had nothing to do with her disappearance, surely he would admit they'd met and simply parted, each going their own separate ways? The Police feared the worst: that Gaskin was responsible for more than simply his wife's disappearance. They began to drag local reservoirs and search the woods. But they had no joy. Their next step was to put more pressure on Gaskin. As he arrived for work on the afternoon shift on the Friday, the Police took him to Cannock Police Station for more questioning. Meanwhile, Mrs Talbot received a note after Elizabeth's disappearance. It began: 'Lizzie is alright. She is with me now. She will send you some money when we get to London,' and was signed 'W Brooks'. But the letter was thought to have been written by Gaskin in an attempt to cover his tracks.

Gaskin continued to maintain that he hadn't met his wife the previous Wednesday. The Police let him sit in his cell and stew. Eventually, on the Sunday, Gaskin asked to see Superintendent Merrey, to whom he made a statement: 'She is in pieces. I cut her head off and tried to cut her leg off, but the sinews held it together.' He told the Police he would take them to his wife's body.

Gaskin led Police first to the woods where he had been seen a few days earlier. He explained that this is where he had killed Elizabeth and attempted to hack the body to pieces. He had also taken a stick that he had rammed down her throat and, once he had severed the head, had rammed a gas-pipe into her torso. He then led them to Victoria Street in Hednesford, to a gas holder tank, and told them that the remains of his wife were in the pond at the of the container. He was immediately charged with murder and the subsequent trial took place on 4 July 1919 at Stafford:

Mr Vachell [prosecuting], in opening the case, said that the story was perhaps more full of horrible details than any story he had ever heard since he had been a member of the Bar. 'There seems,' said the learned counsel, 'to be not the slightest doubt that the unfor-

Victoria Street, Hednesford. It was here that the headless body of Elizabeth Gaskin was found. The author

> *tunate woman met her death at the hands of the prisoner, and the circumstances of that death, the manner in which he killed her, and the efforts he made afterwards to conceal his crime by cutting up her body, are so full of ferocious, inhuman details that it is a task that I shudder at having to present to any jury in the court.'*

Gaskin's defence counsel, Mr Milward, did not try to contradict the material evidence, but made an attempt to persuade the court that Gaskin had not been in his right mind when he committed the murder. Looking at the evidence, it would seem obvious from a modern perspective that Gaskin was not in the best of mental health. Indeed, Thomas Gaskin had a long history of undiagnosed or ill-diagnosed mental illness. As the newspaper records:

> *Mrs Harriett Williams, wife of Henry Williams, mother of the prisoner, was called. She said that prior to the accused's birth she was in a low, melancholy state for 16 weeks. The prisoner had fits*

when a little boy; he was sometimes very passionate and sometimes very quiet. The prisoner never associated with other boys, and was always as a child under medical treatment. On one occasion he tied a scarf round his neck and nearly strangled himself.

Reading between the lines, it would seem that if Gaskin was 'sometimes very passionate and sometimes very quiet' that there was some kind of underlying bipolar disorder like manic depression – it might also be possible that it was a more severe form of illness, such as paranoia or schizophrenia. Whatever it was, it was certainly exacerbated by Gaskin's wartime experience. In 1916 Gaskin had joined the Royal Engineers and was posted to France. It is highly likely he spent a good part of his time in France burrowing in a complex series of tunnels underneath enemy trenches, in order for explosives experts to set mines in place. It was hard, grimy work, without even the rudimentary safety measures of the mines at home, which Gaskin was used to. Tunnel collapses and underground explosions were commonplace. Two of Gaskin's army colleagues testified at the trial that he had not behaved in a normal fashion, and that he 'used to leave the trenches to shoot at bottles and collect souvenirs under shellfire and frequently took unnecessary risks.' Gaskin had also been blown up by a German mine: his sapper comrades, Charles Dawson and Ernest Woodhall, believed Gaskin never fully recovered from the experience. To make matters worse, while he was away at the front, Elizabeth had two children, even admitting that one of them was not fathered by Gaskin (it is unlikely he was the father of either). She had even had her army allowance suspended while the matter was investigated. This could have done little for Gaskin's feelings of security.

At the time of his trial, most people in Britain were still unaware of the true horrors of trench warfare on the Western Front and, unless they had served themselves, could have had little concept of the brutality of the conflict. The men who fought in Flanders did not return home with talk of their experiences and newspaper reporting was heavily censored. Furthermore, understanding the way in which the mind works was in its infancy in 1919. With the benefit of hindsight and

100 years of psychiatry and psychology, it is easy to see that Thomas Gaskin, already suffering from some kind of mental illness, had been badly treated by those who were supposed to love him, and terribly scarred by his experiences as a soldier. He probably needed psychiatric treatment as much as any man ever did. But the prosecuting counsel wanted nothing to do with sentiments and sought the fullest punishment under the law:

> *Mr Vachell said it seemed that the only possible defence was that prisoner was insane at the time he committed the deed. That he did know what he was doing seemed abundantly clear from the detailed account he had given of what he did. He seemed to have justified his acts on the ground that it was vengeance against his wife for the immoral life she had been leading.*

Despite all the evidence that Gaskin was ill, the jury had little sympathy and sided with Mr Vachell: after all, between them they probably knew dozens of men who had fought in the war and who felt no compunction to butcher their wives as a result of their experiences. It took them only 14 minutes to decide that Gaskin was guilty of the crime. One can speculate that the bizarre catalogue of what he did to his wife's body after she was already dead must have outraged the jury and, rather than seeing it as an indication of insanity, saw it as a horrendous act that demanded revenge.

Following his trial in Stafford, Thomas Gaskin was hanged by John Ellis, who was also the executioner for such notorious villains as Dr Crippen and 'brides-in-the-bath' murderer George Smith. The execution took place at Winson Green Prison, Birmingham, on Friday, 8 August 1919. He should not have hanged, but should have been sent to some sort of secure psychiatric unit. But hindsight is a wonderful tool . . ..

Bibliography

Costello, Peter, *The Real World of Sherlock Holmes: The True Crimes Investigated by Arthur Conan Doyle*, Robinson 1991

Cowdell, J. and Tunstall, A., *Policing the Potteries*, Three Counties Publishing 2002

Hitchings, J. and Payne, W., *Stafford Gaol and its Associations with a Record of County Crime and Criminals*, Hanley 1887

Lewis, Dave, *The Rugeley Poisoner – Dr William Palmer, the Prince of Poisoners*, Artloaf 2003

Mackenzie, Compton, *On Moral Courage*, Collins 1962

Nordon, Pierre, *Conan Doyle*, John Murray 1966

Prince, Rosalind, *Capital Crimes: Staffordshire Hanging Offences*, Churnet Valley 1994

Staffordshire Advertiser – various dates

Staffordshire County Council Education Department, *Gaols – Staffordshire study books 1*, Staffordshire 1974

Staffordshire County Council Education Department, *The Case of George Edalji*, Staffordshire (no date)

Staffordshire Sentinel – various dates

The Times – various dates

Thirlby, M., *Life and Death in Prison with Particular Reference to the Gaol at Stafford from 1777–1877*, Dudley Teacher's Centre 1979

Index